If not available at your local bookstore, additional copies of this volume may be purchased for $1.00 from ODYSSEY PRESS, North Road, Poughkeepsie, New York 12601. Please remit payment with order.

# NEW LOOK AT

# EDUCATION

## SYSTEMS ANALYSIS
## IN OUR SCHOOLS AND COLLEGES

# NEW LOOK AT

# EDUCATION

## SYSTEMS ANALYSIS
## IN OUR SCHOOLS AND COLLEGES

### BY JOHN PFEIFFER

THE ODYSSEY PRESS • NEW YORK CITY

This report is the product of a survey sponsored by Educational Testing Service of Princeton, New Jersey.

# FOREWORD

THERE IS A NEW phrase going around education these days. It goes like this—"Now that we have achieved education for *all,* let us seek education for *each.*" It is true that, while this country has reached the goal of universal education, it has yet to provide truly individualized instruction for all our young people.

It is imperative that mass education not become depersonalized education. The child must not become lost in a colossal system of fifty million others, or else we will reap a harvest of dropouts and disenchanted youths on a much larger scale than we have at present.

We have it within our grasp to achieve "education for each," but to do this will call for a newer and higher order of planning than we have so far brought to the process. Educators are exploring more effective programs for disadvantaged students, assessing innovative teaching practices such as audio-visual instruction, team teaching, nongraded schools, programmed instruction, independent learning, and are devising new methods of scheduling classes for more appropriate course offerings for each student. We must go further in accumulating orderly and meaningful school records on pupils, and in using these data for better counseling and guidance in each grade and at each level in the educational process.

Also, with the rising cost of education, we shall need to seek more efficient and productive ways of running our schools and colleges, so that we know more accurately what we are getting for our money as we seek that level of quality which we all desire so much for our children. This is known in the jargon as "more bang for the buck," and, with present expenditures of sixty billion dollars for our schools and colleges, it is a not unimportant consideration.

Fortunately, there would appear to be a way out. Though analogies are never perfect, in the last decade both the military and business establishments, each dealing with people and dollars, have taken a hard look at improved administration, individual productivity, and the cost-effectiveness of their operations, using methods that have come to be known as operations or systems analysis. Quite simply this means that, rather than merely collecting information and statistics on the state of affairs as it is now, data are explored on a wide assortment of choices and alternatives to suggest better courses of action than current practice. The objective is imaginative and effective decision-making, and the steps are three: setting goals; seeking alternatives; evaluating results.

Recognizing the applicability of operations analysis to education, the U.S. Office of Education called a conference in late November 1967 in Washington to which some five hundred were invited. Surprisingly over a thousand attended from schools, colleges, and universities across the country. The discussions of useful applications of the scientific method ranged from site locations of urban schools, to bussing schedules, to measuring student achievement, to the education of disadvantaged children.

One of the most valuable outcomes of these sessions was the dispelling of some myths about the computer as a control instrument over individuals and over the educational process. Basically the computer was put in its proper place, as the handmaiden not the master of education. People still make the final decisions, but wiser decisions based on alternatives rather than a single approach to the solution of a problem.

It must be said that a system does not, of and by itself, produce better education. It should, however, if used seriously, present educators wth the opportunity to face up more exactly to what they want to achieve, a program of how they hope to go about it, and the courage to assess honestly the outcomes of their actions.

This fascinating book deals with the whole subject of how one can be more systematic in his approach to problem analysis, no matter what the enterprise or endeavor—operating a hospital or an army base, establishing flight patterns or controlling traffic flow, or running a school or college. Where other books on this subject lean heavily to the technical or theoretical, this one provides a variety of specific illustrations of the use of systems analysis. It is comprehensive and comprehensible.

I commend this book to all educators, educators-in-training, and even to the layman who, apart from his interest in education, would like to take a look ahead at the promise which lies in the improved methods of planning to meet many of the problems of our society.

*Princeton, New Jersey*     Henry Chauncey, President
*February, 1968*           Educational Testing Service

# ACKNOWLEDGMENTS

THE FIRST STAGE in writing about new scientific developments is to spend time with investigators actively engaged in the experimental process, in the demanding exploration of frontier areas. They provide the information that counts most, not only unifying principles and generalities but also the sharp, precise details which help convey what is actually going on in research.

Such information is particularly important in an introduction to the systems approach. Much of the work in this field is so new, and many of the central ideas are evolving so rapidly, that clear-cut definitions are hard to come by and one must rely all the more on specific examples to indicate some of the basic varieties of systems studies. This book therefore depends more than most on the cooperation of scientists at many institutions.

Among those most deserving of credit is Alfred Blumstein of the Institute for Defense Analyses in Arlington, Virginia, who has thought systematically about the systems approach and who shared his ideas with me. I am particularly grateful for the time he gave me since he was in the throes of preparing a report for President's Crime Commission, a report which represents a pioneering application of systems techniques to a large-scale public problem and thereby opens up new research possibilities in the social sciences in general.

This report, by the way, is also one of the few recent publications including a discussion of the systems approach which nonspecialists can understand and which provides a number of clear examples. (Another such report is the University of Toronto's *A New Tool for Education Administrators*, which is considered in Chapter 6.)

I owe a great deal to Mark Shedd, superintendent of the School District of Philadelphia; and to David Horowitz, associate superintendent in charge of the Office of Planning. They spent the better part of a day discussing some of their problems with Dr. Blumstein, and the discussions helped considerably in giving me a feeling for the subtleties of the systems approach. I only hope they gained as much from this exchange of ideas as I did.

This book leans heavily on the advice of Jerry Kidd of the National Science Foundation who furnished me with an invaluable overall picture of the systems field. He provided guidance as well as information, and, in the process, suggested certain major projects for further research. Some of the investigators consulted took on the extra task of arranging meetings for me with colleagues conducting studies of unusual interest. Burton Dean prepared the way for an extended visit and interviews at Case Western Reserve University. John Coulson, Bertrand Hansen, and Wallace Sinaiko did similar service far beyond the call of duty at the System Development Corporation in Santa Monica, California, the University of Toronto, and the Institute for Defense Analyses respectively.

I am further indebted to a great number of educators and scientists who provided information about their projects or their knowledge of operations which had employed the systems approach. Because the list is long, I have credited their contributions separately in a list which follows this section.

Parts of this book are based on a series of interviews conducted by a fellow science writer and editor, Lawrence Sandek of Nyack, N. Y. He took time out from a most busy schedule to help me during a period when help was needed most.

Very special thanks go to Carroll Newsom and Henry Chauncey for the original idea for the book. They had the feeling that the time was ripe for an introduction to the systems approach, which has been amply confirmed by many specialists in and outside the field. Mr. Newsom also provided partial support for this inquiry by a grant from the Laboratory for Educational Materials. Furthermore, I had the full support of an informal steering committee from Educational Testing Service at every stage of the writing—Scarvia Anderson, Albert Beaton, Harry Harman, and William Turnbull. The book is in a real sense the result of their suggestions as well as those of William Coffman, Henry Dyer, Carl Helm, Frederick Kling, and Wesley Walton.

David Loye and Bruce Taylor shared the all-important task of visiting systems specialists and obtaining fresh information. Additional information-gathering was done by Lois Crooks and Mary Ellen Parry, both of whom exhibited a rare talent for tracking down elusive facts.

I also wish to express my appreciation, with particular emphasis, to John Hollister for his constructive and creative editing, which has contributed notably to the quality of presentation throughout.

This book is, then, in every sense a cooperative venture, and I trust will provide the reader with a broad overview of this interesting new field which has important implications for education.

JOHN PFEIFFER
*New Hope, Pennsylvania*
*February, 1968*

The following educators and scientists were consulted on various aspects of this book, and I wish to record my appreciation to them, at the same time making it clear that they bear no responsibility for the text.

*Wallace Allred*, Brigham Young University Laboratory School
*Leonard Arnoff*, Ernst & Ernst
*Harvey Averch*, The RAND Corporation
*Donald Axelrod*, New York State Budget Division
*Norman Baker*, School of Industrial Engineering, Purdue University
*Howard Ball*, Center for International Systems Research, Department of State
*Joseph Bar*, Buena Vista School District
*James Bassage*, Dade County School District
*Claude Bissell*, University of Toronto
*Martin Blauer*, System Development Corporation
*Joel Bloom*, Franklin Institute Research Laboratories
*Robert Blue*, Buena Vista High School
*Wayne Boucher*, The RAND Corporation

*Samuel Bowles,* Harvard Department of Economics

*Robert Bowman,* Ohio State University Hospitals

*Caroline Boyer,* Case Western Reserve University

*Jack Bratten,* System Development Corporation

*Glenn Bryan,* Office of Naval Research

*Stanley Buchin,* Harvard Graduate School of Business
Administration

*Robert Burden,* Harvard Division of Engineering and
Applied Physics

*Ray Carpenter,* Pennsylvania State University

*Donald Carroll,* Massachusetts Institute of Technology

*C. West Churchman,* Space Sciences Laboratory,
University of California

*John Cogswell,* System Development Corporation

*Peter Czajkowski,* Ernst & Ernst

*William Dill,* International Business Machines Corporation

*Quinton Cramer,* Garber High School

*Alvin Drake,* Massachusetts Institute of Technology

*Richard Durstine,* Harvard School of Education

*Eugene Emme,* National Aeronautics and Space
Administration

*Tibor Fabian,* Mathematica

*Myron Fiering,* Harvard Division of Engineering and
Applied Physics

*Stephen Fink,* Case Western Reserve University

*William Finley,* The Rouse Company

*David Fitzpatrick,* Nova High School

*Gene Fisher,* The RAND Corporation

*Charles Flagle,* School of Hygiene and Public Health,
Johns Hopkins University

*Joseph Froomkin,* Office of Education

*Jack Gebhard,* Applied Physics Laboratory, Johns Hopkins
University

*Thomas Glennan,* The RAND Corporation

*John Golden,* Stanford Research Institute

*William Gorham,* Department of Health, Education and
Welfare

*Charles Halbower,* Arthur D. Little, Inc.

*Wesley Hall,* State University of New York

*James Hardie,* Case Western Reserve University

*Harry Halley,* Office of Economic Opportunity

*Richard Hatch,* Decisions Systems Associates

*Donald Hillman,* Lehigh University

*Robertson Hollister,* Office of Economic Opportunity

*James Hooper,* Case Western Reserve University

*Daniel Howland,* Ohio State University Hospitals

*John Jackson,* Theodore High School

*Donald Johnson,* California State Department of
   Education

*William Jones,* Department of State

*Richard Judy,* University of Toronto

*James Kalish,* Office of Economic Opportunity

*Edward Katzenbach,* Raytheon Company

*John Keller,* University of California

*Herman Koenig,* Michigan State University

*Beverly Kooi,* System Development Corporation

*Luke Krebs,* System Development Corporation

*Norman Kurland,* New York State Education Department

*Richard Lavin,* Raytheon Company

*Ferdinand Leimkuhler,* School of Industrial Engineering,
   Purdue University

*Paul LeVasseur,* Organization for Economic Cooperation
   and Development

*William Levenson,* Case Western Reserve University

*John Little,* Massachusetts Institute of Technology

*Samuel Mantel,* Case Western Reserve University

*Don Marsh,* System Development Corporation

*Bertram Masia,* Case Western Reserve University

*Robert McCambridge,* New York State Education
   Department

*Ronald McDougall,* University of Toronto

*Ronald McKean,* Harvard School of Economics

*William McReynolds,* University of Toronto

*Donald Meals,* Raytheon Company

*Robert Merry,* Harvard Graduate School of Business
   Administration

*John Meyer,* Harvard Department of Economics

*Vernon Mickelson,* Case Western Reserve University

*Donald Miller,* California State Department of Education

*Robert Morse,* Case Western Reserve University

*Charles Mosmann,* System Development Corporation
*Daniel Moynihan,* Harvard-M.I.T. Joint Center for
  Urban Studies
*Joseph Navarro,* Institute for Defense Analyses
*Martin Netzorg,* Ernst & Ernst
*William Niskanen,* Institute for Defense Analyses
*Anthony Oettinger,* Harvard Program on Technology
  and Society
*Maurice Osborne,* New York State Education Department
*Wilfred Owen,* Brookings Institution
*Jack O'Toole,* System Development Corporation
*James Petersen,* The RAND Corporation
*Alan Pifer,* Carnegie Corporation of New York
*Fred Pinkham,* Project Yardstick
*Edward Quade,* The RAND Corporation
*Howard Raiffa,* Harvard Graduate School of Business
  Administration
*Prudence Randall,* Case Western Reserve University
*Gustave Rath,* Northwestern University
*Donald Roberts,* Ernst & Ernst
*Mary Robinson,* Office of Economic Opportunity
*William Schneider,* National Aeronautics and Space
  Administration
*Erno Scott,* New England Educational Assessment Project
*Harry Silberman,* System Development Corporation
*Roger Sisson,* Wharton School of Business, University of
  Pennsylvania
*Marvin Sussman,* Case Western Reserve University
*Daniel Teichroew,* Case Western Reserve University
*Harold Thomas,* Harvard Division of Engineering and
  Applied Physics
*David Tiedeman,* Harvard Information System for
  Vocational Decisions
*Stanley Uchill,* Peat, Marwick and Livingston
*John Walter,* University of Toronto
*Lewis Ward,* Harvard Graduate School of Business
  Administration
*M. Cecilie Watson,* Ontario Institute for Studies in
  Education
*Fred Weinfeld,* Office of Education

*Robert Whorf,* Scientific Research Staff, Ford Motor
    Company
*George Wilkinson,* California State Department of
    Education
*Harry Williams,* Institute for Defense Analyses
*Charles Young,* School of Hygiene and Public Health,
    Johns Hopkins University
*Charles Zwick,* Bureau of the Budget

# CONTENTS

# NEW LOOK AT

# EDUCATION

## SYSTEMS ANALYSIS
## IN OUR SCHOOLS AND COLLEGES

# CHAPTER 1

# A WAY OF THINKING

CAPSBURG U.S.A. (population: 39,104) is a typical American city, which hardly rates as a surprise since that is precisely what it was intended to be. It was planned from the beginning to resemble small cities such as those of the northeastern and north central United States. It has a Main Street, a favorable location along a river, and, like many similar urban communities, a number of serious problems.

Plenty and poverty are to be found in Capsburg. It includes seven residential districts, two of which offer the sharpest contrasts and indicate the sources of the deepest tensions. There is a swank neighborhood with large old houses and ample space around them, high-income families, and an all-white population. Not far away in the center of the city lies a nonwhite slum, where about the same number of people are crowded into one-fifth the area and twenty percent of all employable males are unemployed.

Such contrasts are not unusual in our times. The unusual thing about Capsburg is the simple fact that it does not exist, at least not in the conventional sense.

1

Capsburg is an imaginary city, a "computer city" represented by a deck of punchcards and designed to help investigate the long-range effects of new educational programs on an urban community. The model, which can simulate sixteen years of social change in about four minutes of computing time, is a prototype for studies of the Denver area being conducted by the Colorado Department of Education.

The Capsburg project represents only one example of a development which is already having an important impact on education and other areas, and which promises to have an even greater impact in the years ahead. A team activity known broadly as the "systems approach," it has been hailed by some as a high-powered, high-pressure answer to practically all the problems that plague us today—and belittled by others as nothing but a new jargon for something that sensible people have been doing for decades. In fact, it is neither panacea nor fraud. It is certainly not the last word, but, used within its scope, it can be enormously powerful.

The systems approach can be regarded as a disciplined way of using specialists in a variety of fields to analyze as precisely as possible sets of activities whose interrelationships are very complicated, and of formulating comprehensive and flexible plans on the basis of the analysis. The frame of reference is unequivocally the real world. Formal mathematical procedures may or may not be used, but every case represents a basic effort to reconcile objectives and resources, to achieve clearly specified compromises between what we want and what we can expect to get. In other words, a new service is being developed for planning at all organizational levels. According to one practitioner of the art, "Our trade is to help people make decisions."

Indeed, the systems approach concerns itself above all with the nature of decision making. Intangibles have always played a leading role in the process, and there is no substitute for judgment, the unique contribution of the man shaping major policies. He is always on his own when the chips are down. No one can help him at the moment of decision, when he selects one course of action over another. Before he reaches this stage, the systems approach comes in to provide guidelines and evaluations, on the theory that a combination of his judgment and an analysis drawing on the advanced technology of assessment may be more effective than either alone.

The essential power of the approach is that it offers a solid objective foundation for decisions. It is especially useful when policies and recommendations are to be justified, and in times like ours the administrator is being called on increasingly to account for his plans and substantiate his complaints about limited resources. Under such conditions he finds himself in a position to state his case with confidence and to control more effectively the future of the organization for which he is responsible.

## The Systems Approach to Decision Making

The systems approach is not a set, established thing with clear-cut rules to follow in dealing with all problems. Since it is evolving rapidly and along lines that are not yet entirely clear, the most appropriate strategy at this point may be to convey a general impression only. Later chapters will present a more formal picture, together with examples which are intended to describe the approach in terms of what systems specialists or analysts do, rather than in terms of abstract principles. Generally speaking a systems approach includes the following features or elements:

1) *Design for action.* Scientists have long known that, in research, finding the right questions to ask is half the battle, the idea being that only after you know clearly just what it is you want to learn can you proceed to come to grips with your problem. An analogous principle holds when it comes to shaping administrative policies. The first job in dealing with such problems is to identify exactly what has to be done, which means defining objectives and—more than that—defining objectives in operational terms, in ways that demand concrete action.

Criteria are then selected which measure how well the objectives are being met and determine when those objectives have been reached. This stage of systems analysis depends on the art of expressing aims in specific and economical terms. You may proceed from a vague aim such as "promoting racial relations" to a rather more precise "increasing the nonwhite population of the school," and then to a still more precise criterion: "including at least fifteen percent of nonwhite students in every grade."

2) *Seeking alternatives.* Imagine a meeting held in one of the state capitols to decide whether or not several new state parks should be established. A special staff recommends a clearly defined plan and supports it with charts and slides and tables showing the detailed costs of land purchases, camping facilities, mosquito control, road building, publicity, and so on. The head of the Park and Recreation Department makes his decision on the basis of the staff's recommendations.

For all its care and thoroughness, this sort of presentation illustrates a Hollywood version of sound planning, the old rather than the new way of doing things. It may be systematic, but it is certainly not the systems approach. The missing ingredient is alternatives, and without alternatives the planning staff tends to assume the role of salesman for a particular course of action. The scope of the decision maker's judgment is correspondingly diminished. Secretary McNamara, who introduced the systems approach to the Defense Department, on more than one occasion (and in no uncertain terms) sent planners back to their drawing-boards when they came up with a single-course presentation.

So once objectives and criteria have been determined, the next step calls for identifying and spelling out different methods of meeting each objective. This is an active not a passive step. There must be an organized effort to search out alternatives, perhaps the most important and creative phase of systems analysis. It demands open-mindedness, and readiness to discard preconceived notions. Furthermore, the alternatives may be combined in different ways and each combination represents a possible plan, a set of activities which may bring about a desired set of changes.

3) *Evaluation.* One mark of a really complex problem is that it generally involves a number of objectives not all of which can be fully attained. This means that a realistic plan depends on trade-offs and compromises. The "systems" part of the systems approach comes in most strongly at this stage. A full-fledged analysis will attempt to evaluate a combination of alternatives by maximizing the benefits or utility to be obtained for a given cost, or by minimizing the price which must be paid to achieve specified changes.

Alternatives are generally evaluated in numerical terms, indicating how much money will be spent in a certain period or how many teachers trained or students graduated. But qualitative factors are always to be considered along with quantitative factors; there are always political implications, questions of morale, and other effects, which may not be measurable in satisfactory terms.

Finally, evaluation is a repetitive process. A plan must be monitored to check its current effectiveness, modified if necessary, checked again, remodified, and so on. Continual assessment involves sensitive feedback, cycles of evaluation which permit prompt readjustment of tactics to make sure that the system is moving toward its objectives—a kind of steering by compass.

## Use of Models, Flow Charts, and Simulation

Basic to the entire systems notion is the concept of a model, a simplified but controllable version of a real-world situation which serves a function roughly comparable to that of a laboratory experiment in the physical and biological sciences. More often than not it is impossible to analyze major problems without some kind of model. The problems are far too complex to cope with by ordinary inspection or common sense. We tend to approach phenomena in "linear" terms, as if events always followed one after the other in a direct chain reaction, like the falling of a row of dominoes. Our sentences and our ideas are organized that way.

We might have been able to depend on our own simple capacity for this kind of thinking in a simpler, slower-moving, and less closely-coupled world. But the problems confronting us today involve incredibly complex mazes or "nests" of interconnections and linkages rather than straightforward associations and cause-and-effect sequences, and the results of important changes may be extremely difficult to predict. In such cases a good model can help appreciably by supplementing intuition and judgment. It is one thing to rely solely on speculations about how people will behave under certain real-life circumstances, and something else again when one can objectively investigate possible behavior patterns by simulating those circumstances in a model.

The investigation may make use of a large-scale military exercise at some proving ground, a competitive advertising and manufacturing game played by executives, a simple flow chart indicating the progress of students in a particular course, or an elaborate representation on a computer like the hypothetical city of Capsburg. In any event, the model simulates activities which for one reason or another are either impossible or impractical to carry out in the real world.

Interest in these and other techniques is currently on the rise, and for very good reasons. Preliminary studies indicate that it is time for a comprehensive coming together of the systems approach and education. One factor in the new situation concerns advances within the systems field itself. Although its modern origins may be traced back some three decades, notable developments have taken place recently, during the past five years or so in particular. The systems approach has now reached a new level of sophistication where teams of specialists can provide the administrator with services hitherto unavailable, on a scale appropriate to the problems he is facing.

## New Educational Demands

Meanwhile things have been stirring in the field of education. The demand for more and better education often becomes most urgent in those periods of crisis when we are driven to self-examination and realize most acutely how much we have to learn. It should be no surprise that the demand today is more urgent than ever. Education is being called on to do so much more than it has done before that it is difficult to appreciate the magnitude of the difference. Furthermore, the funds required are being made available for the first time, the ultimate and most telling sign of increased federal concern.

Education occupies a central position in all long-range national planning. It is included in suggested solutions to a wide range of contemporary problems from the population and knowledge explosions to crime and poverty and keeping ahead of, or catching up with, the Russians. Even more significant, it is heavily involved now in the aspirations of the underprivileged of all nations, in the hopes and discontents of people who no longer believe in their hearts that their lowly place in life is part of the natural order of things.

As far as the United States is concerned, one of the critical points in our current phase of renewed interest can be assigned a definite date—October 4, 1957, the date of the launching of Sputnik I. Americans had taken it for granted that man's first artificial satellite would be put into orbit by Americans, and part of the general reaction was shocked surprise and reluctant belief that another nation could surpass us in any aspect of technology. As one consequence, certain statistics which had been known for some time acquired new meaning, namely statistics indicating that the Soviet Union had taken special steps to educate large numbers of scientists and engineers. Another consequence, of course, was an immediate and continuing spurt of activities calculated to improve American education. For example, the rate of instructional innovation in New York public schools more than doubled during the fifteen months following the Sputnik launching.

At about the same time economists in the United States and abroad had been conducting studies which amounted to a broad-gauge evaluation of education.

Education was measured in dollars and cents, the conclusion being that the extension and improvement of teaching paid off because it was a most effective way of increasing national productivity—and, further, that spending money on education brings economic returns at least as high as those of many investments in property and physical capital. Other studies revealed that many plans for economic development were grinding to a halt because of a shortage of specialists qualified to carry them out.

In a sense education has been discovered all over again, in economic as well as humanistic terms, with the steady accumulation of evidence that knowledge is power and knowledge happens to be where the schools are. The evidence is by its very nature politically potent. So the pressure mounts, and from all sides at once. Teacher shortages become more critical as populations increase and chances of keeping up with the accelerating pace of discovery seem slimmer than ever. (According to one estimate enough new information to fill a twenty-four volume set of the *Encyclopedia Brittanica* is added to the world's libraries every forty minutes.) It is not only a matter of teaching more to more students, a sufficiently formidable prospect in itself, but in addition teaching different things in different ways on the basis of individual capabilities and interests.

## New Difficulties in Decision Making

Under such conditions making decisions is a task of staggering dimensions. Every development that shows promise of raising educational standards and the quality of instruction is being put to the test—the increased use of television, slide and motionpicture projectors, teaching machines including specially programmed electronic computers, field trips, intensified teacher training, remedial reading, team teaching, recreation and luncheon programs, individualized instruction. There is certainly no shortage of ideas, and every one of them has dedicated supporters who are convinced that their idea is best and that they have the evidence to prove it.

The big problem is the rising flood of innovation itself, the bewildering array of new possibilities and new combinations of possibilities. In this connection the remarks of the superintendent of a city school system are relevant: "When you get right down to it ours must be a job of synthesis, of putting things together in the right proportions. The way things are now it is almost as if we had car parts but no cars, or at least not enough different models—and no good way of testing a car's performance. Alternatives are coming along so fast that we can't handle them. It's the lack of an instructional systems view that has us blinded."

A significant development is the sudden appearance of big business on the scene. Big business has also discovered education, as an unusually attractive market which offers the chance of combining public service and profits. This active interest is welcome, and will undoubtedly have important and far-reaching effects. But it often complicates the life of the educator who, like the physician trying to choose among the highly publicized products of competing drug companies, must choose among a larger and larger number of devices and materials designed for the benefit of teachers and students. The selection process is made even more difficult by the task of weighing claims and counterclaims and coping with a variety of hard and soft selling techniques.

Pressure is coming from another direction. It may appear somewhat of a paradox that at a time when federal support of education has reached a new high the accent is stronger than ever on economy and strict budgeting practices. But the competition for available funds is also stronger than ever, from all agencies and at all levels of government. This was the main theme of a recent off-the-record meeting. Financial officers representing the campuses of a large and rapidly growing state university attended the meeting at the request of officials in the state capitol.

Details of the proceedings are not expected to be published. But the state's budget director did most of the talking and the gist of his remarks was as follows: "Up to now you've had things pretty much your own way. You've received the funds you asked for, even though you did a poor job of justifying many programs. But from here in things are going to be more difficult. You must develop more effective guidelines and standards." The implication was clear that if the educators did not do a better job of evaluating their programs, others would.

Educators have further reasons to explore and to evaluate the results of their explorations, reasons they share with others in a position to exercise leadership and influence future leaders. Perhaps in part because of their relatively recent exposure to a major depression and two world wars, they are somewhat less certain than they once were about what should be taught and how and to whom. There has been a loss of confidence in the effectiveness of some of the attitudes and dogmas of times past. A loss of confidence can be a positive thing, however. It can lead to a more critical scrutiny of objectives and criteria, which seems to be what is happening.

## Help from Systems Analyses

The systems approach has a role to play in this process, a far more extensive role than it is playing at present. But its impact may be considerably diminished unless we have a clear idea of how it operates and what it can offer, of what it is and what it is not. In the first place there is no such thing as *the* systems approach, if that implies the existence of a formula or a special set of rules for handling problems. A wide range of procedures are available, and which of them will turn out to be most helpful depends on the nature of the problem under investigation.

Teams of investigators are almost always involved, the combined efforts of teachers, psychologists, computer programmers, and other specialists. They may use mathematical techniques of various degrees of sophistication, but they are not primarily mathematicians. They may call on a computer to help them extract meaningful patterns of information from unwieldy masses of raw data or to run model tests, but they are not primarily electronics engineers. The essence of their trade is not a method but a point of view, a spirit of scientific inquiry. They observe and ask questions and gather facts and when the required facts are not available, as is often the case, they see to it that fresh data are obtained. They are continually framing, checking, and modifying hypotheses.

Above all, the efforts of the systems analyst do not mean that education can or should be shaped by experiences gained in economics or industry or military

affairs. An unfortunate tendency is to regard the systems approach as a gift from hard-headed practical
men who are somehow more advanced than their
muddled brethren in education, and are generously
offering the results of their wisdom to a backward
profession. This attitude is implicit in reports which
refer, perhaps with the best of intentions, to the
"education industry" or, even worse, to the "knowledge industry" as if the basic aims of education and
industry had anything in common. To be sure, educators are very much concerned with efficiency and
budgets. But it would be equally incongruous to refer
to, say Proctor & Gamble as a "detergent university"
simply because the corporation is actively engaged in
the training of salesmen, machine operators, and executives. Systems investigators have as much to learn
from educators as educators have to learn from them,
and most investigators know it.

## Planning as a Continuous Process

Finally, use of the systems approach should not be a
one-shot affair in which outside experts descend on a
school or college, do a job, and then depart without
trace for points unknown. Such brief and abruptly
concluded encounters have taken place, and they are
rarely productive. But there is no excuse for them,
even allowing for the severe shortage of qualified
specialists, and some sort of continuing relationship
should be provided for in every contract. The odds are
that in the long run these specialists will have a
permanent place in educational institutions, like counselors and admissions officers.

These and other issues have been widely discussed
during the past few years, and the future will un-

doubtedly see increased discussions. One thing is evident right now, however. The power of the systems approach lies fundamentally in the striking fact that it can promote and amplify incisive thinking. As has been indicated, it has a way of bringing problems into more intense focus, primarily by identifying and defining objectives in operational, action-oriented terms. From one point of view it may be regarded as a major step in applying the scientific method to the art of getting things done.

Incidentally, there may be an interesting relationship between our increasing emphasis on the need to define objectives and our increasing experience with computers. Computers are notorious for their simple-mindedness, among other things. They demand instructions spelled out in excruciating detail, and dealing with them has probably forced us to become more explicit and exact in dealing with one another. We can be brilliant but rather sloppy thinkers; computers are stupid but accurate. It seems that during the course of time, in the evolving symbiosis between man and machine, we are destined for better or for worse to become somewhat more precise (and, of course, the computer will inevitably become somewhat more intelligent).

The coming together of the systems approach and education is by no means an isolated phenomenon. Viewed in broad perspective, it may be seen as part of a significant shift in social values. The nation has long ranked Number One among nations as far as telephones, automobiles, and other possessions are concerned, while achieving rather lower ratings in such things as medical care, education, and crime control. Now we are beginning to take these matters seriously in a new and more determined way. One sign of the trend is the fact that the systems approach, which until recent times has been applied chiefly to military and industrial problems, is now beginning to enter the picture not only in education but in all other so-called "public" areas—in all major projects involving health, welfare, economic opportunity, urban renewal, crime, poverty.

So a report on the systems approach and education must be to some extent a report on changes in national outlook, in our notions about what is important and unimportant. The following chapters discuss the history of the approach, its use in areas other than education as well as in education itself, and possible future developments. It should be emphasized that the book is introductory rather than comprehensive, presenting some examples of studies under way at some institutions. The aim is to convey a general feeling for certain new techniques and attitudes which may be of value when it comes to translating ideas and plans into action in the field of education.

# CHAPTER 2

# DECISION MAKING IN ACTION

THE SYSTEMS APPROACH arose in response to the same demands which brought about the development of radar, rockets, nuclear weapons, and antibiotics. It is an outgrowth of procedures developed by professional teachers for professional fighters during the early days of World War II. Teams made up mainly of biologists, mathematicians, and physicists were mobilized from classrooms and laboratories to help design software instead of hardware, plans instead of equipment, first in the Battle of Britain and later in all major campaigns. They used their methods of learning, rather than their specialized knowledge, in the cause of improving military tactics and strategies.

Their work justified itself from the very beginning. There were a great many ways of improving air defenses in the Battle of Britain—selecting the most favorable locations for fighter bases and radar installations, providing increased training for pilots and maintenance crews, establishing better communication and control systems, and so on. The problem was to determine the best "mix" of these alternatives, taking the fullest advantage of radar and other innovations and allocating limited resources as efficiently as possible while the enemy mounted his attack. The job was accomplished with the aid of half a dozen professors attached to Fighter Command. Decisions based on their analyses doubled the chances of fighter planes intercepting Nazi bombers, thereby in effect doubling the power of the Royal Air Force.

Another early study led to notable successes in the air war against submarines, to the surprise of many military experts who agreed with Admiral Doenitz, Commander-in-Chief of the Nazi U-boat fleet: "An airplane is no more an enemy of the submarine than a crow is an enemy of the mole." One famous analysis ran directly counter to the established practice of dropping depth charges set to explode a hundred feet beneath the surface, indicating that a shallow setting of twenty to thirty feet would prove far more effective. The change was made, after some opposition, and increased the number of U-boats sunk by more than fifty percent.

The lesson of these and subsequent investigations was not forgotten when the fighting stopped. They had demonstrated for the first time on a large scale that something new and extremely significant is created by the establishment of a working relationship between decision maker and systems analyst. The decision maker can act on his own, as he often must during a war and other emergencies; indeed, under such conditions his experience and judgment may provide the only basis for action. But whenever possible he should also draw on the systems approach, because sometimes even intuition can go wrong. (For example, the policy of setting depth charges for deep detonation in air attacks actually reduced chances of destroying a submerged U-boat to about one in a thousand, thus practically insuring the submarine's escape.)

## Program Budgeting, RAND, and McNamara

The approach evolved rapidly after the war. It was applied to broader and "sloppier" problems involving greater uncertainties, more complex mixes of long-range defense-attack strategies, and objectives which were difficult to define. One phase of the systems approach, known as program budgeting, was to receive special attention in Washington. Program budgeting may be regarded as a way of organizing cost data in such a manner that they can be used to analyze different courses of action in terms of cost and utility. Program budgets indicate specific purposes and methods of carrying them out, in sharp contrast to conventional budgets which indicate general categories only and tell little about plans and objectives.

For example, a conventional federal transportation budget might include a "Water transport" category and list under it the requirements for the Department of Commerce, the Coast Guard, and the Interoceanic Canal Commission. "Aviation" and "Highways" categories would be broken down in similar fashion. A program budget, on the other hand, would cut across formal organizational lines and show precisely how and why money is to be spent. One major category might be "Improve intercity transport," and expenditures for various innovations in aviation, highway design, and water transport might all be listed under that heading.

An analogous budget for a school system or university would emphasize programs of instruction, special as well as regular programs, and the facilities and plans proposed for future improvements in each program. Furthermore, like all program budgets it would look ahead five to ten years instead of only a year or so as in conventional budgets. It should be pointed out that the conventional budget, which generally involves such major categories as maintenance, transportation, supplies, and salaries, also has its uses for legal and practical reasons. With its emphasis on objectives and alternatives and precise evaluation, however, program budgeting is expected to see wider use as the systems approach is itself used more widely.

The history of program budgeting may be traced back twenty years to the "performance" budgeting of the Hoover Commission for Reorganization of the Executive Branch and, before that, to studies of public administration conducted during the 1930's and earlier. But the most intensive and original applications after World War II were made under military auspices, particularly at the Air Force sponsored RAND Corporation in Santa Monica, California. In fact, the organization recommended program budgeting to the Air Force as early as 1953, and the suggestion was received with what has been officially described as "something less than complete enthusiasm."

Enthusiasm and acceptance came seven years later when Secretary McNamara met Charles Hitch, one of RAND's leading exponents of program budgeting, and invited him to help reorganize planning and budget procedures at the Department of Defense. Hitch accepted, bringing with him several of his RAND associates as well as a number of analytical techniques for evaluating plans and strategies, the objective being to get the most out of given and limited resources. One of the first important jobs of the new team was an analysis of an Air Force proposal for an additional wing of B-52 bombers and the production of nuclear powered B-70 bombers equipped with Skybolt rockets. By the fall of 1961 Secretary McNamara had received a set of reports which indicated that alternative measures might meet future strategic demands more effectively, and he took immediate action against production of the bombers.

These and subsequent studies have had a great influence on the shaping of the nation's military policies—the shift of emphasis from bombers to missiles, the reduced vulnerability of deterrent forces, the increase of tactical air forces in Army divisions. In almost every case the prospect of change aroused concern and opposition, as it always does, but this did not discourage attempts to assess the comparative costs and effectiveness of doing things differently. In other words, the decisions finally arrived at were based on calculated trade-offs and the weighing of alternatives as well as on individual intuition and judgment.

The success of such procedures was striking. Indeed, it was so evident that in the summer of 1965 the White House issued an executive order to the effect that from then on measures like those used in the Department of Defense were to be used in evaluating programs proposed by other federal offices and agencies. One result, of course, has been to establish the systems approach as a matter of national policy. Even more significant, the order represents official recognition of the fact that in a fundamental sense civil rights, the war against poverty, and other nonmilitary issues have attained an urgency comparable to that of military programs, which after all is something new.

## A "How To" Approach for Educators

This may be a good point to take a closer look at things. As the systems approach comes into prominence, educators and others will have increasing occasion to consider it in somewhat greater detail. We have already emphasized that they will not find a clear-cut set of rules or a step-by-step framework constructed along do-it-yourself lines. We would be proceeding under false pretenses if we presented the approach as other than a thing in process, rather fuzzy at the edges perhaps, but embodying a core of procedures which can be identified and used to good effect.

The rest of this chapter is based largely on discussions with Alfred Blumstein of the Institute of Defense Analyses in Arlington, Virginia. Recently he served on the President's Commission on Law Enforcement and Administration, known as the President's Crime Commission, as director of a special task force organized to indicate how science and technology can play a far greater role in combating crime than is the case at present. The report of the task force emphasizes possible contributions of the systems approach, and during the study Blumstein became increasingly aware of the value of the approach in education, among other areas.

At a meeting held in the spring of 1967 Dr. Blumstein participated in discussions with Mark Shedd, superintendent of the school district of Philadelphia; and David Horowitz, associate superintendent in charge of the office of planning. During the course of the discussions he outlined a version of the systems

approach which is essentially that outlined in the
following paragraphs. It covers a whole range of procedures from defining the problem and basic objectives to the selection of one of a number of courses
—all part of a sophisticated and disciplined way of
thinking about plans and alternatives.

Defining the problem is almost a stylistic thing,
calling for a certain simplicity of design. It is to some
extent a pruning and clearing and lopping-off operation, an intense effort to eliminate trivia and secondary
issues, and to concentrate on basic relationships. It
means obtaining a clear picture of the dimensions of
the problem, understanding the rules of the game—
and that may not always be as easy as it sounds. It is
actually a complex procedure which includes four
distinct phases.

1) *Defining the system's objectives.* Sometimes a
project can bog down or fail completely because the
planners decided on the wrong objectives. To cite only
one example the effectiveness of naval defenses increased enormously early in World War II when it was
decided to concentrate on protecting Allied shipping
and sea lanes rather than on sinking U-boats (the original major objective). A poorly chosen or poorly defined
objective can nullify the efforts of the best administrators.

2) *Obtaining measures of effectiveness.* Measuring
the wrong things may be as unproductive as selecting
the wrong objectives. Appropriate yardsticks are essential to setting goals, making improvements on schedule,
and keeping tabs on how closely the schedules are being
met.

3) *Identifying constraints and uncontrollable variables.* Since every system is part of a larger system,
there will always be things that do not change and can-

not be changed in any reasonable period. These are known as constraints and range from fixed budgets and existing rules and laws to firmly established traditions which serve a real purpose or which have little value but are not yet ripe for breaking. Uncontrollable variables include things like the weather and population trends, which may indeed undergo spectacular changes but are not normally under the decision maker's control.

4) *Identifying controllable variables.* The decision-maker is naturally concerned above all with introducing innovations and hastening or slowing the pace of events, with those elements which he can change "to order" in his efforts to get results.

Once the boundaries of a problem have been clearly marked out, the emphasis is on planning possible courses of action. Every problem has a number of subobjectives or subfunctions which must be considered in the process of achieving the major objective. Furthermore, there are generally a number of different ways of carrying out each subfunction and of bringing it into a better relationship with other parts of the total system. An important part of the systems approach is to specify the subfunctions and the alternatives, and then to build them into total systems which can be evaluated and compared in terms of basic objectives.

For example, suppose the major objective of a public safety program is to reduce traffic accidents. One might define three subsystems: the drivers, the vehicles, and the highways. As far as improving the driver is concerned, accidents might be reduced by punishing traffic violations more severely, administering more frequent eye examinations, requiring more training at driving schools, and so on. Less powerful engines, more thorough factory inspection, dashboard padding, and antiglare windshields are among the ways of making cars safer; while highway safety features include properly banked curves, larger and more frequent signs, and improved lighting.

Many subsystems can be built from all these factors and they must be investigated if we want to learn which combination of driver, automobile, and highway characteristics will result in the fewest accidents (assuming, of course, that for various reasons not all safety steps can be taken). The process as outlined so far may be represented in the following diagram:

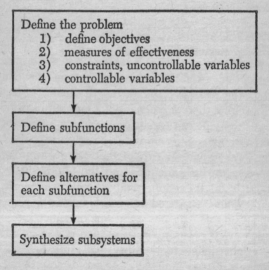

Define the problem
   1)   define objectives
   2)   measures of effectiveness
   3)   constraints, uncontrollable variables
   4)   controllable variables

Define subfunctions

Define alternatives for each subfunction

Synthesize subsystems

Table 1 indicates in a rough way how the systems approach has actually been applied in the analysis of four situations. Although synthesized subsystems are not included, the variety of possible combinations is evident. The antisubmarine example has been taken from reports on the development of strategies in the

TABLE 1. SOME SYSTEMS APPROACH ELEMENTS

| | Antisubmarine Air Patrol 1940 | Air Traffic Control 1960 | Criminal Apprehension 1967 | Urban Education 1970? |
|---|---|---|---|---|
| Objective | destroy submarines | prevent collisions | decrease crime | improve education, esp. of students in lowest socioeconomic bracket |
| Measures of effectiveness | probability of sinking, number of flying hours per kill, etc. | probability of collision, delay, cost | probability of apprehension, time from crime to police arrival at scene | proportion graduating from high school (current proportion: 20% of the lowest quartile) |
| Constraints and uncontrollable variables | weather, submarine characteristics, range and speed of planes, etc. | weather, traffic load, reaction times, etc. | speed of patrol cars, limitations on search, calls for police service, reaction times | state curriculum requirements, student enrollments, salary regulations |
| Controllable variables | intelligence operations, number of planes, technological changes, etc. | separation of planes, technological changes, etc. | technological changes, number of complaint clerks, number of police cars, etc. | technological changes, extracurricular programs, programs for parent involvement, location and size of schools |
| Subfunctions | detect submarine; destroy submarine | detect plane positions; generate control orders; communicate orders | detect crime; dispatch police to scene of crime; travel to scene of crime | forecast future needs; provide teaching staff; transmit information |
| Alternatives | detect: radar, visual, magnetic devices, patrol destroy: mines, depth charges, rockets | detect: radar, visual, pilot reports orders: time separation, distance separation communicate: flashing lights, voice radio, radio signals to auto-pilot | detect: patrol units, alarms, victims and witnesses dispatch: public callboxes, radio networks, dispatchers, computer command and control travel: patrol cars, helicopters, scooters | forecast: pop. trends, political pressures, technological changes provide: mix of teachers and teacher aides, inservice training, teacher-student ratio transmit: conventional classrooms, individual instruction, computer-assisted learning |

North Atlantic. The air-safety example is based on a
study published in 1960 and discussed at the meeting
with Mark Shedd and David Horowitz. The police-
arrests study is part of the 1967 report of the President's Crime Commission. Finally, the example involving education is only preliminary, being included to
indicate future possibilities.

## Developing Systems Analytical Models

This is not the full story, of course. The diagram on
page 24 represents only a bare outline of what actually goes on. In its present form it does not include
the use of a model, which is essential not only to the
systems approach but also to any scientific effort to
understand events. A model has an interesting and
significant double aspect. As has already been pointed
out in the last chapter, it is an abstraction—a highly
simplified version of a fragment of the real world
which is too complex for us to deal with directly. At
the same time, however, it is one highly effective way
of coping with reality.

Subsequent chapters discuss a number of models in
some detail. Here we shall simply emphasize certain
limitations and advantages, and the general role of
the model in the context of systematic inquiry.

For example, scientists recently made use of a
miniature earth, a magnetic steel sphere about the
size of a softball. They placed it in a sealed vacuum
jar, produced an intense electric field such as might
be caused by sunspots, and created a bluish circle of
light over the sphere's north pole—a small-scale northern lights display. This experiment is part of a long-
range study of the upper atmosphere in general, and
of spacecraft communications blackouts in particular

since auroras may interfere with radio reception. It happens to involve an obvious physical model. But models can be of varying types and of varying degrees of abstraction. An experiment may be designed to investigate the effects of a new drug on cancer cells, the behavior of rats in a maze, or the primitive chemical conditions under which life on earth may have originated. The investigator selects as his model some narrow aspect of the real world and subjects it to carefully controlled changes, which will hopefully produce effects that are significantly related to effects in the real world at large.

The same expectation applies to more abstract models, such as those consisting of mathematical equations, which express simplified and formal concepts about natural phenomena. In any case a model is meant to clarify, and to yield information. That depends on how well it is designed. It will certainly be modified or superseded sooner or later in the light of accumulating knowledge, which is the general fate of models. Indeed, from one standpoint the role of a good model is to speed its own obsolescence. It cannot provide final answers and is not intended to. It has served its purpose if it provides fresh insights into the working of things.

In the systems approach the development of a model proceeds along with the already outlined steps leading from the definition of the problem to the synthesis of subsystems. The first version may be merely a rough flow chart indicating the sequence of these steps, like the diagram earlier in this chapter. That version, and subsequent refinements of it, serve, among other things, to indicate gaps in our knowledge and point toward the sort of data needed to fill the gaps. This is a most valuable function. There is no more futile activity in science than the dogged accumulation of facts in the hope that meanings will somehow arise spontaneously once a certain critical data mass has been achieved.

So the development of a model calls for and guides the collection of data. There can be nothing superficial or perfunctory or remote about this phase of the process. People working in the systems field speak of "grubbing around in the data," which means just what it says—digging down to the roots of things, searching out, getting your hands dirty. The investigator must go where the action is, into the schoolroom or hospital ward or jail or battlefield. He must often make something of a nuisance of himself by asking questions and more questions, until he discovers what people do not know as well as what they do know.

## Flow Charts and Models

The data must be gathered, organized, analyzed, and then used to evaluate—often by cost-benefit studies—innovations and the combinations of innovations included in alternate subsystems—which is just where program budgeting may come into the picture, together with an assortment of related techniques. These added steps may be represented in a more detailed version of our previous diagram as shown on page. 29.

This is a fuller but still incomplete flow chart, and the missing element represents a basic characteristic of the systems approach. The act of selection is shown as the end of a step-by-step process, when it should be the beginning—or, more accurately, it should be regarded as part of a cyclical and continuing process.

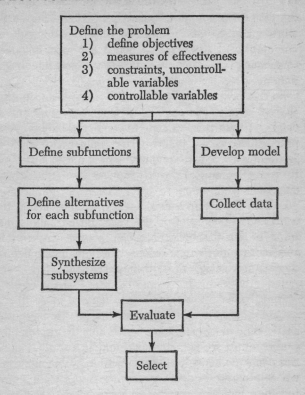

The preparation of an initial study—defining alternatives and subsystems, building models, and analyzing data—may result in a selection as indicated in the diagram. But more often than not the evaluation itself leads to further studies, which eventually lead to further and more sophisticated selections.

The systems approach must prove itself by predicting results reasonably well. It says in effect that if you take a certain course of action certain things will happen, and on occasion it may predict with impressive accuracy. Military experience provides one notable example of success forecasting, again involving air patrols against submarines during World War II. This time the analysis concerned operations in the Bay of Biscay and indicated that two submarines would be sunk per week if twenty-five extra bombers were added to the patrol. After some argument the bombers were provided reluctantly for a trial period of three weeks, during which exactly six submarines were destroyed.

It would be convenient if all outcomes could be predicted as neatly. But the case of the submarine patrol is one that permits rather precise studies because, although there is definitely a human element, it involves machines and other physical devices predominantly—and it has been observed that the combination of a man and a machine behaves more like a machine than a man. In other words, precise forecasts are possible in any situation which, like that prevailing in the Bay of Biscay campaign and in certain industrial contexts, leans heavily on the use of machines in carrying out its operations.

Precise forecasts are rare in more complex military and industrial situations, and even rarer in education, health and welfare, and other public areas. The systems approach reflects the fact that uncertainty increases inevitably as machines become less important than the human element, that a certain amount of sloppiness is part of the nature of all vital and evolving things. This is why selections must be tentative and why the predictions upon which they are based must be checked and re-checked.

## Refining the Model

The problem is how much the model is off, how much it departs from reality—and the deviation demands new analyses to provide more realistic, more precise, predictions. That means re-examining assumptions at all levels, along the subsystem-alternatives-subfunctions and data-model channels, and discovering and making appropriate changes. It may even be necessary to make changes at the uppermost level to transform an uncontrollable into a controllable variable or devise new measures of effectiveness or re-define objectives. All this means readjusting models, new evaluations, and new selections as the feedback cycle proceeds. So our final flow chart, with feedback channels included, takes the form shown on page 32.

An enormous amount of experience and trial and error has gone into the development of such procedures. "The critical art in the beginning," Blumstein emphasizes, "is knowing where to truncate or cut short, where to avoid side issues and bring your thinking to bear on the really important and interesting controllable variables. These variables are our levers on the real world; we can first manipulate them in our model world and see what happens. Then we are better prepared to organize the real world and make things happen there. We are creating structures."

The systems approach is one of the newest and most rapidly evolving phases in man's attempt to make order out of chaos, or near-chaos. We seem always to be teetering on the edge of complete catastrophe; indeed, there is at least a fighting chance that we

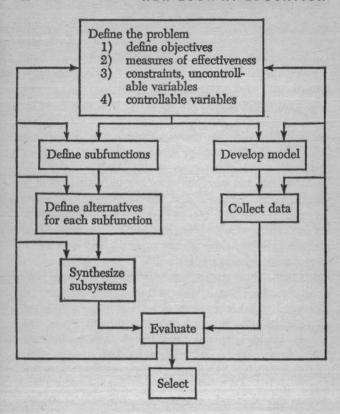

may yet achieve complete catastrophe. But if we manage to avoid it, it will be because we have learned to deal in a disciplined manner with our biggest problems, to impose a rational structure on phenomena whose structures are not immediately apparent. In this effort the systems approach will assume increasing prominence.

# CHAPTER 3

# VARIETIES OF PROBLEMS

SINCE THE USE of the systems approach in education is a relatively recent development, new and preliminary studies in this field may best be viewed against a background of what has already been done in other fields. This chapter indicates the nature of some representative problems, the richness and variety of methods available to deal with them, and a number of practical results. It will be evident that definite educational implications exist, that educators are not alone but are being called on to consider many critical questions which have arisen in other fields as well.

Speaking from a broad systems point of view, there are three general types of problem (with considerable overlapping, of course). First of all, there are the well structured problems which involve relatively clear-cut objectives, quantitative information that may not be too difficult to obtain, and in many cases a single best solution. They can often be analyzed with the aid of established mathematical techniques. There is also another type of more "personal" problem which places a greater emphasis on the judgments and intuitions of experts, on nonquantitative or semiquantitative information, and on special techniques to get at such information. Finally, as we have already pointed out, the most problematical problems of all are found in the public area. They tend to be characterized by a multiplicity of objectives many of which have not yet been defined, a shortage of information, and a certain confusion as to just what information is actually required.

Among well structured problems are those which call primarily for what mathematicians refer to as "constrained maximization" or, to put it in more simple terms, getting the most out of limited resources. Indeed, it is a matter of record that the most spectacular successes of the systems approach in the Department of Defense and elsewhere depend more on the strategic use of maximization methods than on any other factor. Mathematicians have developed a variety of such methods, most of them highly technical. But the basic principle may be illustrated by a rather straightforward example: a science department chairman in a high school has an assignment problem involving five teachers and five subjects—general science, biology, chemistry, physics, and earth sciences.

Imagine that each teacher's ability to teach each subject has been rated according to a scale where 1 represents "very poor," 2 "poor," 3 "adequate," 4 "good," 5 "very good," and 6 "excellent." For example, teacher A is very poor in general science, adequate in biology, poor in chemistry, adequate in physics, and excellent in earth sciences. The other teachers have been similarly ranked, and the total information can be presented as follows:

|          | General Science | Biology | Chemistry | Physics | Earth Sciences |
|----------|-----------------|---------|-----------|---------|----------------|
| Teacher A | 1 | 3 | 2 | 3 | 6 |
| Teacher B | 2 | 4 | 3 | 1 | 5 |
| Teacher C | 5 | 6 | 3 | 4 | 6 |
| Teacher D | 3 | 1 | 4 | 2 | 2 |
| Teacher E | 1 | 5 | 6 | 5 | 4 |

The problem is to assign one teacher to each subject so as to make the best overall use of the teachers. Obviously you cannot take the ideal step of assigning every teacher to the course for which he is best qualified, because teachers A and C are both best in earth sciences, and the rule is one teacher for one course. Furthermore, you have little choice with teacher D who is good in one subject only, and far more choice with C, the best all-around teacher. So a compromise must be arrived at, a compromise which achieves a pattern of optimum use.

To solve the problem you follow a rule which can be learned in half an hour, calls for some elementary arithmetic, and yields the answer indicated below (the teachers selected being indicated by the ratings enclosed in circles):

|          | General Science | Biology | Chemistry | Physics | Earth Sciences |
|----------|-----------------|---------|-----------|---------|----------------|
| Teacher A | 1 | 3 | 2 | 3 | (6) |
| Teacher B | 2 | (4) | 3 | 1 | 5 |
| Teacher C | (5) | 6 | 3 | 4 | 6 |
| Teacher D | 3 | 1 | (4) | 2 | 2 |
| Teacher E | 1 | 5 | 6 | (5) | 4 |

Notice the nature of the compromise. Three teachers have been assigned to their second-best courses, and two to their best courses. But looking at the assignment pattern as a whole, every class has a teacher whose rank is at least "good" (4) on the scale.

## The Place of the Computer

Before turning from this simple hypothetical example to more elaborate studies of actual problems, the matter of time required for calculating should be considered. The teacher problem involves a so-called five-by-five matrix, and a procedure which in effect is a short cut method for selecting the best assignment pattern out of 120 possible patterns. Using paper and pencil, the calculations should take five to ten minutes at most, which does not represent a major effort. But even so there is no reason to do the calculating if one has convenient access to a computer.

A common arrangement is a teletype-machine terminal located in a corner of the office or laboratory and connected by telephone circuits with a large computer which may be a few miles or many hundreds of miles away. Communicating with the computer merely requires dialing a number, flipping some switches, and typing a code indicating the program to be used, the raw data, and a billing number. The computer starts typing the answer almost before you finish typing the question, and it is worth consulting even for problems as simple as that of the five teachers, because people make errors far more frequently than computers.

Of course, computers are indispensible in dealing with more complex problems. For all that has been written about them, it is difficult to appreciate their power. Perhaps the critical fact is that today's fastest models are some one to two million times faster than a man at a desk-type adding machine, which is about the difference between a day and a millenium and means that studies are being undertaken routinely that were unthinkable less than a decade or so ago. A problem with a ten-by-ten matrix, say assigning ten persons to ten positions, involves selecting the best of 3,628,800 possible patterns. It could be done using paper and pencil, but the first attempt would take a few hours and you might spend as much time again finding and correcting errors. The number of patterns for a twenty-by-twenty problem is astronomical, about 25 hundred million billion or 25 followed by seventeen zeroes, and computers have been used to handle much larger matrices.

Considering these facts it is not surprising that investigators, including computer specialists who should know better, sometimes become mesmerized by hardware and behave almost as if they expected the computer to do their thinking for them. To avoid just such temptations the director of one systems group has established a general rule: "I strongly discourage any member of our group from using a computer until he has sized up his problem thoroughly, and decided on the best way to solve it. Then he can come to the machine for detailed calculations." (Certain exceptions to this rule will be considered later.) In other words, ideas must come from people, and computers can be tremendously powerful tools in exploring some of the implications of the ideas.

### The Johns Hopkins Story

A real-life example will indicate how the computer

and the assignment technique can be used in a systems approach. More than a decade ago the Johns Hopkins Hospital formed a so-called operations research group to investigate its activities from a systems standpoint. Headed by Charles Flagle, an experienced systems specialist, the group launched a broadly conceived research program which is still expanding and has served as a model for other hospitals and medical centers. Its current activities include studies of comprehensive patient care and the keeping of complete medical records (the records for any given person are likely to be scattered and inaccessible when needed), decision problems involved in diagnosis and treatment, and the application of management techniques to hospital administration.

One of the early phases of this program was connected with the shortage of nurses and the most efficient use of available personnel. The work started with an examination of current policies, and a significant redefinition of objectives. Instead of trying to maintain a full nursing staff in all wards at all times, whether or not the wards were full, it was decided to adjust the staff to daily patient loads. This led to an intensive analysis which could easily be the subject of a book in itself. It meant a study of all the duties of head nurses, assistant head nurses, general staff nurses, licensed practical nurses, nursing aides, and ward clerks (in order of decreasing salary)—what they actually did as well as what they were best qualified to do. The two are not always the same, and highly trained persons were often spending a disproportionate amount of time doing what less skilled persons could have done at least as well.

Patients were also observed closely and divided

into three categories depending on the amount and type of care they required: self-care, partial or intermediate care, intensive or total care. To obtain this information nurses kept detailed records of ninety-six patients for four days, twenty-four hours a day. Then assignment models were set up, on the basis of matrices which involved a row consisting of the six nursing-staff positions, a column of fifteen or more duties, and the costs of using various types of personnel to perform each of the duties.

A computer helped solve specific problems. For example, one study indicated that a staff of two head nurses, two licensed practical nurses, four nursing aides, and one ward clerk would be required to provide optimum care for a ward consisting of twelve self-care, eleven intermediate-care and three total-care patients. One of the interesting things about this suggested staffing pattern is that it does not jibe with the notion that a group with a single head or leader is necessarily the most efficient arrangement for all situations. Judging solely by what has to be done, and not by the conventional man-at-the-top hierarchy, the requirements of this particular situation dictated two head nurses supplemented by a group of rather less highly-trained assistants. (Notice that the analysis called for no assistant head nurses or general staff nurses, the two next most highly trained workers after head nurses.)

It should be clear that this is only a very small part of a major investigation by Flagle and his associates, Robert Connor, Harvey Wolfe, and John Young. But the use of such assignment models is changing one aspect of nursing practice. Assignment patterns are calculated daily and used to determine nursing-staff distributions for one of the clinics at the Johns Hopkins Hospital. Other hospitals have turned to similar models in working out their own problems. The relevance to a variety of educational situations is obvious, particularly in connection with current teacher shortages. How, for example, could one make the most effective use of teachers and counselors and teaching and counseling assistants.

## RAND and Los Angeles School Bussing

Another study involves somewhat different mathematical techniques but the same general problem. In the Los Angeles school system, as in the school systems of many other large cities, marked inequities exist in the distribution of classroom space. There are some schools with vacant classrooms and others, predominantly in Negro areas, where overcrowding is severe. About five years ago a group of parents formed a private foundation and organized a daily bus service to make use of some of the unused space in elementary schools. This service includes about half a dozen schools and brings more than two hundred students from crowded to uncrowded areas.

In line with a plan to extend this service and have it supported by public rather than private funds, a team of mathematicians and political scientists at the RAND Corporation investigated the situation for the foundation. The Los Angeles Board of Education has a rule that transfers may be made to schools having two or more vacant classrooms, and at the time of the study there were 55 such schools with places for 2370 pupils. The objective was to fill as many of these places as possible, taking account of the following constraints: 1) no child should be transported more than fifteen miles and the distance should be minimized, and 2) the cost of the program should also be minimized.

Such problems demand a certain give and take. The aim is always to obtain the best overall solution in a world where not everything is possible. In assigning the five teachers to five subjects, for example, it was not possible to have each teacher working in the course for which he was best qualified. Similarly, in the Los Angeles transportation problem it was not possible to fill every one of the 2370 vacancies and at the same time minimize travel distance and costs. Incidentally, this case illustrates how the same research principle may underlie a variety of apparently unrelated problems. The RAND investigators found that an existing model of mathematical equations— which had already been used in such applications as helping a local gas company install pipelines for most efficient fuel distribution—would also work in the routing of pupils.

The solution required a few seconds of computing time. It indicated that for a cost of $259,880, or less than seven percent of the annual transportation budget, and a maximum travel distance of 14.8 miles all but 210 of the 2370 vacancies could be filled. This would be the equivalent of adding 72 classrooms to the school system. The plan also included a complete schedule indicating how many pupils would be picked up at each of 42 bus stops, specified optimum bus capacities, and dealt with a number of other factors.

The story does not have a happy ending, at least not yet. It can best be described by a statement sometimes made in connection with another problem: the operation was a success but the patient died. The study is recognized as a first-rate job technically. But it ran head-on into a wider social problem, a not uncommon occurrence which will be discussed more fully in a later chapter and which illustrates the point that every system is part of a larger system. The Board of Education, which had not yet completely formulated its racial integration policies, turned the plan down. But the vote was a close 4-3, and it is hoped that the approach may be applied at a future date in Los Angeles and elsewhere.

## Marine Corps Matching of Men and Jobs

A larger-scale allocation problem concerns military policies, and has aroused enthusiastic support rather than opposition. One of the most prevalent and widely protested facts of life in the Armed Forces is that men are on occasion assigned to positions which have little to do with their preferences or abilities. Indeed the complaint is so common that the men themselves fatalistically tend to regard it as an inevitable part of the military system. But the situation has improved considerably during the past few years.

In the spring of 1964 the Office of Naval Research decided to go ahead with a preliminary computer project to be carried out at the Marine Corps recruit depot in San Diego. For a long while the Office had been considering various ways of matching men and jobs more efficiently, and the decision to concentrate on this particular project was well timed for technological as well as other reasons. Significant advances had recently been made in computer design. The latest machines were not only faster than ever but, even more important, their memories had been increased to the point where they were capable of storing well over half a million "bits" of information, which is the information content of about a thousand pages of fine print.

Speed and large memory capacity were needed because of the magnitude of the problem. A computer was to take account of the test scores and interview results of a large group of recruits, assign them to different schools and training centers, and evaluate the assignment pattern. Furthermore, the machine was to keep on making assignments and evaluating new overall patterns until it arrived at a pattern which could not be improved on, which ranked as the best possible man-job match. Richard Hatch of Design Systems Associates, a Maryland operations research firm, worked out an appropriate computer system, modifying a procedure originally developed by RAND scientists.

After about fifty trial runs, the system was ready for its first full-scale task, a problem involving about 5000 Marine recruits and 150 different kinds of jobs. To arrive at an optimum solution the computer tried a total of more than 100,000,000 man-job matches, comparing the qualifications of each man with the prerequisites for each job. The calculations, which would have taken thousands of years using a desk-type adding machine, were completed in less than three minutes. As an outcome of similar projects computerized assignment systems are now being used regularly by the Army and Navy, as well as the Marine Corps.

Measures of effectiveness are one of the basic features of the systems approach, and these procedures are definitely paying off. Former methods involved a so-called clear-the-desk strategy. Assignment officers, working under pressure with lists of positions that had to be filled in a hurry, examined batches of say fifty to a hundred records, and did their best to figure out some sort of good matching. Their problem was not only that the mind cannot cope with such a large number of possibilities, but also that their time perspective was extremely narrow. They were making assignments on an immediate basis without knowing what sort of recruits would be coming in the next week or what sort of positions would be open.

So the old "manual" methods generally yielded limited results. In one comparative study of 2500 Army assignments, personnel officers using such methods succeeded in placing only about one out of every seven or eight men in an occupation which he preferred. For the same 2500 men the computer method was about four times more efficient, placing better than one out of every two men in a preferred occupation. The computer performed the added task of minimizing transportation costs by assigning men at the various boot camps to the nearest advanced training bases, thereby saving about $3,000,000 a year in travel expenses. Furthermore, since computer methods achieved an improved match of aptitudes and jobs, there was a marked increase in the proportion of men completing their advanced training.

These results indicate the value of allocation-of-resources studies in which many alternatives must be considered. The accent has been on such studies, because they are of basic importance in the systems approach and because they have direct relevance to many problems in education (although educators can expect clear-cut optimum solutions in rare cases only). There are other problems, however, which at the most fundamental level may be related to the allocation of human effort, but which demand different techniques and a different sort of perspective.

## PERT and Critical Path Methods

One sign of the times is the greater and greater complexity of getting from one place to another, establishing and meeting schedules, and regulating the flow not only of materials and finished products but also of all sorts of activities and ideas. What we do in our jobs and when we do it depends more than ever before on what others have done or should be doing, and our work today determines the work that others will be doing in many places tomorrow. In other words, we all function as parts of more and more elaborate networks, and our effectiveness relies increasingly on the quality of studies designed to influence the pace and order of events.

A simple example may be used to introduce the science of scheduling. Suppose that in a five-step process the first two steps A and B may be performed simultaneously, steps C and D depend on step A, and step E depends on steps A and B and C. This sort of structure may come up in making parts in a machine shop or arranging a meeting or planning a trip, but whatever the context it can be represented by the following network:

Suppose further that step A takes 40 minutes, step B 20 minutes, and step C 25 minutes, step D 20 minutes and step E 15 minutes. The information can be incorporated into a more complete diagram:

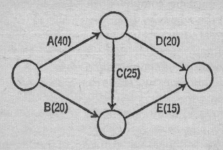

One of the first questions that can be asked of such a diagram is how long the entire task will take, what is the longest way through the network. In this case direct inspection points to the sequence A–C–E which takes a total of 80 minutes and is generally indicated by a heavy line:

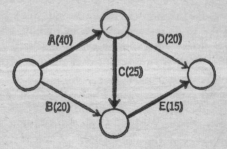

A–C–E is called the critical path. It has a special significance in that it focuses attention on those steps which determine the completion time of the process. Steps B and D are "slack" steps which allow some leeway and need not be strictly monitored; B, for example, could take as long as 65 minutes without delaying the overall process. If you want to meet your schedule, however, the critical-path steps A, C, and E must be completed on time—and if you want to beat the schedule, these are the steps to streamline.

A great deal of research has been done on the critical-path method, and on many variations and refinements of a related method known as PERT (Program Evaluation and Review Technique) which deals with cases where completion times are uncertain. The unaided brain was never meant to cope with real-life schedules and networks which may involve hundreds or thousands of intricately interrelated steps or activities. Du Pont engineers pioneered in developing critical-path methods during the mid-1950's, and one of their most effective studies reduced idle equipment time in a synthetic rubber process by more than thirty-five percent and increased annual production by about a million pounds.

Today such techniques are applied widely. They have become standard practice in the construction industry, and the federal government requires all contractors to "PERT" their schedules. State University of New York planners not only require critical-path schedules from contractors bidding for new jobs but also hold special meetings beforehand to describe the new methods to would-be bidders. PERT has even been used to schedule a play, including some 200 activities from the completion of the script and the hiring of a director to the search for backers, arranging rehearsals, and booking a theater for opening night in New York. (The play, a comedy, failed and never reached Broadway—another indication of the limitations of the systems approach, which cannot pass on matters of taste or the quality of judgments.)

Many of these studies involved computer programs. But computers are not strictly necessary for handling all processes of say fifty to several hundred activities, and special methods have been devised which do not depend on electronics. The computer is absolutely necessary, however, when it comes to the analysis of supernetworks. In fact, PERT was developed to coordinate the several thousand activities required in the Navy's Polaris missile project and is credited with helping complete the project two years ahead of time. The largest networks yet analyzed—those concerned with the production of new automobiles, rockets, and manned space vehicles—may be made up of as many as 20,000 to 30,000 different activities.

More dynamic networks, involving unpredictable and often eccentric flows of equipment, characterize modern traffic conditions. Since problems of this sort are intimately connected with the population explosion and the growth of cities, they can rarely be handled as isolated phenomena. But precise analysis is possible under certain limited conditions such as may be found among cars moving through tunnels, where policemen are omnipresent to enforce regulations and there is no passing.

## Traffic and Transport Studies

General Motors and Port of New York Authority engineers have investigated traffic flow in the Holland Tunnel with the aid of a so-called follow-the-leader theory. The theory has been derived from extensive observations carried out and analyzed over a period of years. One finding is that a driver generally begins to interact with the car ahead of him when he approaches to within about 200 feet, and that he interacts primarily by gauging his speed relative to that of the other driver. Mathematical equations based on such information have yielded some fairly accurate predictions. For example, the equations predicted that maximum traffic flow would occur at a speed of nineteen miles an hour, and studies of actual flows indicated that the figure was 18.2 miles an hour.

Further analysis concerned the tendency of cars to bunch up. A driver moving along at a steady pace suddenly slows up perhaps to take a look at the scenery or because he has underestimated the steepness of a hill and has to downshift. The car behind has to follow suit—and soon a whole flotilla of cars may be moving bumper to bumper. It was found that such bottlenecks could be reduced by letting traffic into the Holland Tunnel in batches. Whenever forty-four cars entered the tunnel in less than two minutes a policeman held up the following cars until the two minutes were up, a policy which increased traffic flow by about six percent and decreased breakdowns by twenty-five percent because there was less stopping and starting.

Far more complex situations arise when it comes to cars moving on city streets. According to John Little of the Massachusetts Institute of Technology, who is especially interested in traffic-light systems, such situations demand extremely elaborate analysis: "If you were driving alone on a street, it would be possible to synchronize the lights so that whenever you reached an intersection the light would turn green. For one-way traffic, this is a fairly trivial problem. But if you consider both directions at once it becomes much more difficult, and it becomes still more difficult if you consider heavy traffic. Ideas that work at low flow do not necessarily work as you get more cars on the street, and you must begin to worry about how traffic on one street relates to traffic on all other streets."

Little and his associates are using mathematical theories or models to study and eventually improve traffic flow in Boston, San Jose, and other cities. Other studies, particularly those conducted under the direction of John Meyer at Harvard, having been concerned with urban systems requiring combinations of railroad, automobile, and bus transportation. Although neat predictions and confirmations are not possible at such levels of complexity, it has been encouraging to note that the results of mathematical work are sufficiently realistic to check reasonably well with actual traffic experience.

## Library Information Retrieval Systems

Mathematical techniques have also been applied to the field of information retrieval, to the task of coordinating and keeping track of and using the expanding store of human knowledge. Among the leading groups concerned with problems in this vast area is that headed by Ferdinand Leimkuhler of the School of Industrial Engineering at Purdue University, where library systems have been under intensive study for a number of years. There are concrete "hardware type" problems such as determining the most compact way of storing books, which is another form of the familiar process of making the most out of limited resources, and there are broader problems in which the subject of study is the entire library-user environment and the development of a mathematical model of a university library.

A representative study, which Leimkuhler reported at a recent New York meeting of systems specialists, makes use of techniques related to those developed for antisubmarine defenses during World War II. By the time a destroyer reached the scene of a sinking ship, the submarine had often submerged and left the immediate area. But its underwater speed was sluggish compared to that of the destroyer, a fact which made it possible for mathematicians to devise search theories and extremely effective ways of finding U-boats. If a destroyer executed various specified maneuvers, spiralling out from the scene of the sinking in ever-widening sweep paths, it would have a high chance of finding the submarine with sensitive sound detectors and destroying it with depth charges.

Since the war, theories of searching and target detection have been applied to methods of prospecting for oil and other industrial projects—and Leimkuhler has found similar theories helpful in analyzing problems of tracking down references in libraries. He proposes a special plan for going through scientific literature, a plan based on the finding that two thirds of all desired information is provided by only about fifteen to twenty percent of the documents in a given field. In other words, a search should begin with these most productive documents, and the rest of the material should be consulted later if the first search fails. These and similar studies are bringing the problem of library organization into sharper focus. They support the notion of a massive storage place for at least seventy-five to eighty percent of all material, plus an active center for the rest of the material, the material most frequently referred to.

Another concept is taking shape at Lehigh University. During the past five years Donald Hillman of the Center for the Information Sciences has been developing a basic theory of information retrieval which involves network and lattice analysis and other mathematical models—and has been designed to achieve a unique kind of conversation between man and computer. The objective is to provide an informal computerized service for specialists seeking information, even if they go about it unsystematically. As Dr. Hillman has said, "It is a mistake to assume that a person necessarily knows what he wants to know."

A kind of pilot service has recently been demonstrated at Lehigh. The user has access to a specialized library of 2500 documents—which, by the way, are devoted to information retrieval and storage—through a teletype machine wired to a computer. He can type out a question in ordinary English rather than in some computer language, and the machine recognizes its basic meaning whether he types, "I would like an introduction to the problem of information retrieval—something not too technical," or, "Can you refer me to a simple book about information retrievals?" The machine provides the requested references and may ask questions of its own or make suggestions, and Hillman plans to refine and extend the service as experience accumulates.

This is a partial survey of some problems which have been solved or better understood with the aid of established mathematical procedures. They are precise problems, not only in the sense that the objectives have been clearly defined, but also in the sense that they involve situations or aspects of situations in which people are obeying rules and trying to behave in a comparatively predictable fashion. But notice the price one pays for precision. As a rule it means a relative narrowing down, even in the systems context. As we confront wider problems we approach border-lines where things tend to be rather blurred, our theories are less well developed, and we rely increasingly on efforts to find quantitative and empirical relationships in the judgments and experiences of decision makers.

# CHAPTER 4

# PEOPLE AND JUDGMENTS

SOME RATHER STRANGE games have been played at the Institute for Defense Analyses. But even a visitor in the know would have been startled if he had overheard a telephone conversation under way one day in the fall of 1964. A man was shouting something to the following effect: "You can forget that plan as far as my country is concerned! I've told you for the last time that we'll back you up in a showdown! But you can be sure of one thing. We're not going to go broke because of a threat that may come to nothing!"

The speaker was not a diplomat who had lost his calm. He was one of twelve college students located in twelve different offices and participating in a game called "CRISIS," in which each student represented one country of a major alliance. The alliance faced the threat of a sudden attack from a powerful enemy, and the objective was to decide how much each country should contribute to a mutual defense fund. It was only a game, but every phase had been carefully planned to make it as realistic as possible. Real stakes were involved, poker chips or cash representing a nation's resources; time was running out and the pressure was on. The participants certainly behaved as if they were playing for keeps, judging by the excitement, heated arguing, interruptions, and angry flareups.

The study had been set up more than a year before partly as a result of the efforts of Jerome Wiesner, then White House science advisor and now provost of the Massachusetts Institute of Technology. Dr. Wiesner was concerned with a kind of hot-line notion applied to alliances made up of many nations, (except, of course, that the U.S.–U.S.S.R. "hot line" is actually a teletype system). He suggested a research project devoted to the question of whether in times of international emergency the heads of state and their representatives could settle problems on a rush basis and at a distance, without waiting to arrange face-to-face meetings.

The White House gave the study a high priority rating, and soon a "teleconferencing" project had been established. Experimental work was assigned to a team under the direction of Thomas Belden and Wallace Sinaiko of the Institute for Defense Analyses. Alex Bavelas, a Stanford University psychologist who had conducted basic studies of group behavior, served as a consultant. Their work furnishes an excellent example of the systems approach as applied to a problem about as far removed as possible from the problems considered in the last chapter. Those problems are essentially of the classical type. They involve familiar principles such as search and assignment patterns, have been studied for years, and can draw on an established body of mathematical analysis and theory.

## CRISIS and Teleconferencing

Teleconferencing is something else again. It represents another class, another world, of problems. There are the personalities and intense emotions of individuals who are committed and acting under tension, who have axes to grind and causes to promote. Indeed the investigators themselves had to operate under some tension, because the project was to be completed within six months and solid evidence was scarce. They developed the game of CRISIS as part of a broad experimental program devised to obtain information about the variety of alternatives.

The student shouting into the telephone was playing one version of the game, the so-called "party line" version in which any one of the twelve participants could speak up whenever he wanted to. According to one Institute report, things often became hectic under such conditions: "Negotiations were intense and moderately chaotic, although . . . not quite extreme enough to break down the discussions. It seems likely, however, that groups of more than twelve members would tend to break down the party-line network." (Seato, Nato, and the United Nations are made up of 8, 15, and 122 member nations, respectively.)

A second alternative was an "automatic successive broadcast" network, in which a person could keep talking until he stopped for three seconds. At that point a tone signal would start, and the first of the eleven other participants to signal for the line would get it. This system, which was not actually tried with the twelve-man group because it proved so unsatisfactory with smaller groups, had two major drawbacks, both of them related to the fact that the speaker could

talk as long as he wanted to without being inter-
rupted. It encouraged the universal and overpowering
tendency to be charmed by the sound of one's own
voice and resulted in long-winded talking which was
not always to the point. Also, crisp give-and-take
discussions were difficult because a player with a
question or an idea that could open up a new approach to a problem might have to wait five minutes
before getting a chance to talk and by that time his
remark might have little impact.

The third and best alternative was a network controlled by a chairman, a player who sat in front of a
panel (in effect a telephone operator's switchboard)
on which a light appeared for each player who
wanted to speak. The chairman could decide who
would speak next and could also request comments
from players whose interests were involved but who
had not signalled. As might be expected, this system
resulted in orderly and relatively fast negotiations;
players finished the game within an hour, compared
to two or more hours for six-man groups using the
successive-broadcast system.

## Games for Resolving Social Conflict

Belden, Sinaiko, and their colleagues explored a
great many other situations. They studied more than
thirty-five groups in all, varying in size from two to
twelve members, and learned among other things that
the party-line arrangement worked best when only
three persons were involved. At the other end of the
scale, it became increasingly difficult to recognize the
speaker by his telephone voice alone, so that special
recognition arrangements would certainly have to be
made for very large groups. This problem would be

more serious in top-secret sessions using voice-scrambling devices to prevent outsiders from listening in. After the messages are unscrambled, they are easy to understand but have a Donald Duck quality which makes it impossible to recognize the speaker even though you have known him all your life.

Different types of communication were compared: face-to-face conversations, written messages delivered by intermediaries, teletype and telephone networks, and various mixed procedures. Under the informal conditions of the experiments, which included scientists and businessmen as well as students, it made little difference whether the conferees spoke face-to-face or over the telephone. This was a surprise, since it suggested that a technically difficult combination of television-type screens and telephones might not be necessary (although the screens would clearly solve the speaker-recognition problem in large group teleconferences).

Written messages raised some special problems, over and above the fact that they took two to four times longer than face-to-face talks and telephone conversations. There seems to be something about the very process of writing which works against the spirit of flexibility and compromise. The language used in the written messages tended to be formal and stilted and dogmatic, a sign of rigidity in thinking and attitude. The conferees behaved as if the act of putting themselves on the record made them reluctant to change their positions, and they frequently exhibited a "historical bias," referring back to previous notes instead of shaping their remarks to fit the tone and direction of current discussions.

In connection with this phenomenon, one series of

particularly interesting experiments suggested that when persons with conflicting opinions try to compromise or reconcile their differences using teletyped messages they do little conceding. On the other hand, when they try compromising by telephone results are far more satisfactory. It should be emphasized that writing showed up as a relatively poor way of communicating under the particular conditions of this experiment. Under a variety of other conditions writing has a number of important advantages. For one thing we can all talk faster than we think, so if time permits us to put our ideas in black and white the result is generally a clearer and more disciplined presentation.

The teleconference project also yielded some insights into the psychology of conflict. Arguments rarely flared up when two partners in an alliance started with equal or nearly equal resources, say 35 poker chips for one and 40 for the other. They regarded one another as equals and had little difficulty deciding on their shares of the mutual defense fund. A very poor partner also had no trouble reaching agreements with a very rich partner, since he had little to lose anyway and his share was necessarily more of a token than a substantial contribution. Moderate differences, rather than extreme or negligible differences, tended to produce the most frequent and most heated arguments, for example when one partner had 50 chips and the other 25.

Another major phase of the project concerned the use of official languages in international meetings. Special emphasis was placed on the speed and accuracy of interpretation, a problem which becomes particularly important during a crisis. The most widely publicized incident involved the phrase "We will bury you," which Soviet Premier Khrushchev used in a speech referring to the United States and which the press widely misinterpreted as a thinly veiled military threat. Literally the phrase means just that. But while it is not exactly chummy, it is a common Russian saying which has no connotations of fighting or killing and simply means, "We will be around when you are gone."

Investigators studied the frequency and nature of interpreters' errors, the effectiveness of bilingual teleconferences, and other aspects of the language problem. During the course of this research they discovered that an interpreter, a specialist trained to translate directly from the spoken word, could be used to scan teletype messages in French as they came off the machine and read the English version aloud—with few and relatively minor errors. Furthermore, he could produce the English version seven times faster than a specialist preparing written translations from the teletyped messages.

The report on this and related research, which was completed early in 1964, has not produced any dramatic policy changes. But events continue to underline the need for international teleconferences or some other type of formal system in case of emergency, and the project has stimulated related work in a number of industrial laboratories concerned with satellite communications. Moreover, the Department of Defense has conducted further experiments on the use of interpreters to translate teletyped messages at high speeds, while the Institute itself applied certain findings to a classified study of networks involving larger numbers of people.

Viewed as a whole, the teleconference project illustrates the systems approach to a problem for the analysis of which few standard techniques exist. The problem was unusual but its objectives were fairly clear. So were the major subobjectives and subsystems involved in designing the best possible communications network with the best possible interpreting methods. Not only that, but little doubt existed as to the strategy of the study, considering time limitations. It was a probing sort of study conducted to discover some of the sensitive variables, the variables which could be changed to produce the greatest effects. A great deal was learned about relative values of different sorts of networks under many conditions.

A great deal was learned, and a great deal remains to be learned. At one level it would be important to have more empirical data—to know more about larger groups of say 50 to 150 persons, the uses of television devices and other hardware, the effects of interpreting in several languages, and so on. At a deeper level we have yet to understand the basic elements affecting group communications under normal as well as under tense conditions. What is lacking above all is a predictive theory of social behavior, and the most significant advances await developments along these lines. In such a context it makes little sense to speak of solutions. It is a matter of preliminary recommendations and suggestions for further research.

## Games and Models

Notice how CRISIS was used in this study. Models, as we have said earlier, may range from the relatively realistic to the highly abstract, and within this spectrum games obviously have a place. The most realistic models are full-scale operational exercises, dramas acted out with all the props and atmosphere of actual events. Policemen chase and shoot blank cartridges at colleagues playing the roles of criminals; naval units do mock battle with one another on the high seas. At the other extreme the most abstract models are the mathematical variety, including equations that represent theories of search, target detection, assignment procedures, and so on.

Games occupy an intermediate position in the spectrum. Less realistic than operational exercises and less abstract than equations, they still preserve some of the gadgetry of real-life situations as well as the human element in the form of people confronted with dilemmas and making decisions. They may be devised for amusement or training or to give administrators a feel for the intricacies of current problems. (War games of various sorts, for example, have long been used at the Pentagon, where the players include members of the Joint Chiefs of Staff and high-level civilian officials.) In this report, however, our concern is exclusively with games as one of the tools which may be used in the systems approach.

Again it should be emphasized that many modern applications have been stimulated by the demands of war. One of the earliest systems games was played more than twenty-five years ago in connection with the Bay of Biscay maneuvers of British air patrols against Nazi submarines mentioned in Chapter 2. The successes in that campaign depended in part on a game played on a large chess-type board with pieces representing submarines and radar-equipped aircraft. In more recent times the composition of Army divisions operating in Southeast Asia, the proportion and roles of helicopters and associated equipment, has been based on the judgments of military experts as indicated by the way they played specially designed war games.

## Games in Educational Settings

As far as education is concerned, game playing has not yet been used extensively in the systems approach. Most studies have been conducted to teach high school students rather than to analyze educational problems. For example, the Western Behavioral Sciences Institute at La Jolla, California, has designed games in which students assume the roles of legislators and deal with medicare, tax reduction, antipoverty programs and civil rights. Hall Sprague of the Institute believes that such games are "to the soft sciences what a laboratory is to the hard sciences of physics, chemistry and biology" and that they provide "a gut-level understanding of the pressures that go with a position of power." The odds are that sooner or later systems studies will involve teachers and school administrators in games designed to provide insights into the nature of essential educational problems and, like the teleconference game, to indicate the sources of conflict and cooperation in communications.

Techniques of another sort are being developed which can be expected to come to the aid of educators struggling with apparently unlimited alternatives and limited budgets. Although such cases demand a rational allocation of resources, they cannot make use of mathematical techniques such as those described in the preceding chapter—and the reason is fundamental to an understanding of the broader, more "personal" applications of the systems approach. In assigning nurses, for example, the variety of duties can be specified, and the costs of each duty calculated precisely and objectively. But accuracy cannot be expected in situations which rely heavily on human judgments or matters of opinion; and where accuracy is uncertain standard mathematical techniques are of very limited value.

There is at least one effective way to make use of the ideas and informed guesses of experienced persons. Part of the trick is to sit down and begin spelling things out, which is what people always do when the time comes for getting down to brass tacks—and in addition to put evaluations in quantitative (if only approximate) terms. The painstaking process demands a steady and relentless effort to pin down statements. The systems investigator must ask first whether a certain course of action is good, then whether it is better than another course and, if so, better by how much according to some arbitrary rating scale, in a continuing round of questions and tentative decisions.

## Establishing Priorities

The Department of State, for example, has experimented along such lines in connection with its cultural and educational program. The total budget for the program is made up of the individual budgets for offices in every one of more than a hundred different countries, and each of these budgets is made up of items rated more or less important on the basis of our objectives in the particular country. In other words, the overall program is a complex of priorities and of priorities within priorities—hierarchies of judgments representing the subjective values of many persons who have had long and firsthand experiences of conditions prevailing in the different countries.

More than two years ago the Department's bureau of educational and cultural affairs decided to investigate the use of the systems approach in determining the mix of bureau activities which would benefit foreign policy most for the least cost. Fundamental to this approach is the distinction between choices arising in day-to-day operations and longer-range planning decisions. Planning decisions that involve allocation of resources can be based on probabilities, average relative effectiveness, and other readily measured concepts. But operational choices are extremely difficult to put in quantitative terms. For example, there are few precedents for measuring the relative value of sponsoring a tour by *Hello Dolly,* the Woody Herman band, or the Cleveland Symphony; giving a grant to an American chess champion or a lecturer in hematology; assisting one African student in political science or another student in agricultural chemistry.

A preliminary study concerned the subprograms for six countries: Argentina, Cambodia, Japan, Pakistan, the Philippines, and Tanzania. Bureau officers compiled a complete list of all benefits, in terms of the improvement of relations among nations, that had been observed to result from cultural and educational exchange activities. The list included "gaining or maintaining access to hard-to-reach peoples, societies, or groups"; "strengthening access to and influence among actual and potential leaders"; "enhancing respect for the democratic political institutions and ideals of the United States"; and a dozen other possible benefits. Then the officers compiled another list of more than thirty-five possible ways of achieving these objectives and the average cost of each activity —the cost of sending an American sports team abroad ($5,585), supporting a foreign student in the United States ($2,863), providing a scholarship in an American-sponsored school ($691), and so on.

Subsequent steps dealt with the effectiveness of each activity with respect to each benefit, and the value of each benefit in promoting the relations of the United States with each country. For example, "strengthening access to and influence among actual and potential leaders" might be regarded as quite important in the Philippines, of intermediate importance in Japan, Pakistan, Argentina, and Tanzania, and of less importance in Cambodia. "Gaining or maintaining access to hard-to-reach peoples" might be considered of major importance in Cambodia and less important in the other countries. Each judgment, and there were hundreds of them, received a numerical rating.

In all their work the program planners put their experience on the line. They had no formal rules to guide them, no equations or theories developed as a result of previous studies of a similar nature. They presented their cases, listened to different evaluations, and kept at it until a consensus was achieved in every case, an exhaustive and exhausting process. Systems investigators at the Franklin Institute Research Laboratories in Philadelphia participated in the process and then designed a set of computer instructions or a model to perform the calculations required to determine the best mix of activities for each country.

A subsequent study of ten countries provided an index of the validity of the model, the degree to which it checked with actual evaluations and decisions. Trial computer runs were impressive. They produced programs agreeing with programs produced by State Department planners in a majority of judgments. The computerized system has not been adopted. However, it has served as a useful preparation for more systematic, noncomputerized management and plannings systems for the exchange program.

## The Harvard-ETS "Harbets" Model

Efforts to get at the nature of human judgment are also involved in a number of cooperative projects between industries and educational institutions, projects in which the accent is primarily on the decision maker himself rather than on his decisions. For example, in 1955 Educational Testing Service and thirty-odd companies began a long-range investigation of how to improve the selection and development of executives. In a key phase of the investigation the Harvard Graduate School of Business Administration participated in the shaping of a program that combined the two general procedures described so far in this chapter, a computer model and game-playing.

The final version of the model described the total operations of a Massachusetts company specializing in the manufacture of grinding wheels and known as "Harbets" (an acronym for *HAR*vard *B*usiness school and *E*ducational *T*esting *S*ervice). This model was completed by Stanley Buchin about six years ago. In building it he gathered an enormous amount of data to prepare a program of instructions for a large general-purpose electronic computer. Harbets had to specify detailed rules which in effect told the machine precisely what arithmetic steps to follow in deciding when overtime work was called for, when more employees had to be hired and how many and at what salaries, how long it would take to find and train employees, and so on. The model included about 10,000 such rules. It took about twenty minutes of computing time to carry out the 4,000,000 program steps required for the simulation of a year's operations. (Today's faster machines could probably do the same amount of calculating in less than five minutes.)

The business game was played on the model over periods of eight days by teams of four men acting the roles of vice presidents in charge of manufacturing, sales, research and engineering, and finance. Each day represented three months of company operations under various conditions of supply and demand and competition, and each day called for a number of activities—handling problems arising from daily in-basket messages, holding conferences and telephone conversations, and making decisions based on new developments and on reports from the computer showing results of decisions made during previous days.

The Harbets project data have not yet been analyzed completely, but it is already evident that a number of findings are relevant to problems of executive behavior. For example, teams made up of experienced executives did much better than amateurs, an observation which was to be expected and tended to reinforce confidence in the validity of the model. More specifically, the decisions of experienced executives almost always resulted in improved operations from day to day, which was rarely the case among the amateur teams. In fact, more often than not the amateurs' new decisions made things worse; they would have achieved better results if they had not changed their decisions at all.

The emphasis on basic investigations of group behavior will become greater as the systems approach is applied to problems of wider and wider scope, to those in which politics plays a major role. Although politics is found everywhere, it rarely reaches a high pitch in such matters as determining the best search patterns in antisubmarine warfare, the workings of a telephone network, or the relative values of different activities in a cultural program. Politics enters in full force in the public area where there is a tendency to defend or attack with great vigor objectives which are often conflicting and ill-defined.

Yet the demand for systems research in the public area is certainly on the rise. It comes largely from Great Society programs at the federal level and, at the state level, from such developments as California's "aerospace contracts" in which four aviation companies were selected to prepare preliminary analyses of waste management and pollution, transportation, communications among intrastate agencies, and crime and delinquency. There is a getting-on-the-bandwagon aspect to all this, as organizations hitherto devoted almost exclusively to military or industrial studies begin to show a new interest in government and the public welfare. About two years ago professional systems analysts were probably spending about ten percent of their time on such work, but the figure may already have doubled and further increases are on the way.

## The Indus Plain Study

The public area involves all the complications encountered in other areas, only more so. There are not only big problems but batches of interrelated big problems, each of them including many alternatives. In addition it is important (and very difficult) to conduct follow-up studies, to avoid the one-shot study and to make the systems approach part of a strenuous and continuing effort. A notable case in point is a survey of the water resources of the Indus Plain in West Pakistan which started in the fall of 1961 as the result of a White House directive.

A "computer task force" consisting of fifteen scientists under the direction of Robert Burden and Harold Thomas of Harvard's division of engineering and applied physics, spent two years on one of the most complex and important systems studies undertaken to date. Harold Thomas has described the origin of the project: "The Administration had been deeply concerned with the unfavorable image of the United States that had been formed in other countries—an image of the enormous potential for destruction by nuclear war. President Kennedy wanted very much to find a dramatic example of the great potential for peace and abundance that inheres in our technology and the will of our people."

The problem was to restore the productivity of one of the world's great river systems—the Indus River and its five major tributaries, each larger than the Colorado River, which have nourished towns and cities since prehistoric times. For more than fifty years leaks have been developing in the 10,000-mile network of canals which links the rivers and irrigates the Indus Plain. The leaks have caused the ground water table to rise until many places which were once farmlands are swamps and lakes; in other places fertility has declined with the increasing concentration of root-damaging salts due to rapid evaporation from the surface. As a result, some 100,000 acres of farm-land are ruined every year.

The value of computer models is particularly evident in the approach to such problems. At one time investigators might have decided to construct a physical model, a kind of small-scale landscape gardening project complete with water flowing along concrete runways to represent miniature rivers, dams, and canals. In fact, about a generation ago Army engineers actually built a 200-acre physical model of the entire Mississippi watershed as part of a flood control survey. Now many structures may be specified in full detail without going to the trouble of building physical models. Computer models, conceptual systems consisting of instructions coded on punchcards and describing hypothetical experiments, are far more flexible than physical models; structures and experimental conditions can be changed simply by changing the instructions.

The basic computer model for the Indus Plain study was used to simulate various ways of lowering the water table—drainage ditches, sealing the leaks in the canals, sinking tube wells into the soil to pump out the water. The final plan, which was completed in 1963, recommended a grid of thirty-two thousand wells covering an area of about twenty-five million acres. It is also specified that each phase of the work should involve an area of at least a million acres, because for smaller areas water seeping in from neighboring regions would replace much of the water being pumped out.

Recent reports indicate that the computer model tests can be translated into full-scale engineering projects. About two million acres of land have been recovered to date, enough to feed four million persons, and water levels seems to be falling at about the predicted rate of a foot or so a year. The problem for the future is one of continuity: whether enough momentum has been built into the plan so that enough pumping stations will be built to revitalize the entire area, and whether further recommendations will be acted on—the building of an electrical power network, and the use of fertilizers and pesticides and other measures. The success of the broad program depends on the extent to which initial studies are followed up. Similar conclusions apply to model studies of the Aswan Dam region on the Egyptian Nile, the irrigation pipeline running from the Sea of Galilee in Israel, and Vietnam's Mekong River basin.

## Prototypal Crime Commission Models

The overriding importance of built-in momentum, of taking special pains at the very beginning to insure that what has been started will be carried through, is recognized in another major investigation. In its 1967 report *The Challenge of Crime in a Free Society* the President's Crime Commission has recommended that systems research groups "be established in the larger criminal justice agencies" as one way to "infuse science and technology directly into day-to-day activities." The Commission also conducted several preliminary systems studies, under the direction of Alfred Blumstein, to indicate the sort of thing that could be done on a larger and more refined scale.

One of the studies has already been mentioned briefly in Chapter 2. It concerns the speed with which criminals are apprehended and is related to the time which elapses between the placing of an emergency call and the appearance of police at the scene of the crime. Analysis of data obtained from the Los Angeles Police Department revealed that this time averaged 6.3 minutes for cases which were never cleared and 4.1 minutes for cases which ended in arrests, indicating that one desirable objective might be to reduce the response time.

So the Commission designed a mathematical model of the apprehension process, a "Capsburg" of a sort. As described in punchcard form the hypothetical computer city had a population of 500,000 persons distributed over an area of a hundred square miles (which is about the population density of Atlanta or Indianapolis). The city also had 1000 callboxes which its citizens could use to telephone the police, 40 one-man patrol cars, and two or three clerks to answer and route emergency calls. The model made it possible to ask the computer the following kinds of questions: How much would the total response time be reduced for each additional patrol car? (Answer: four seconds.) Which is a better investment, spending $50,000 for one extra patrol car or spending it for 1000 extra callboxes? (Answer: add the car, which will reduce delays by at least twice as much as the callboxes.) In other words, the model was providing precisely the sort of cost-effectiveness analyses which are used in program-budgeting procedures to arrive at optimum allocation of resources.

The Commission concluded that the best measure from the standpoint of time reduced per dollar spent would be to introduce a computer system into the police communications center, and the next best measure would be to add another complaint clerk if the staff included only two clerks. (If there are already three clerks, adding a fourth would be practically useless.) "These results apply directly only to the hypothetical city," the Commission points out, "but they suggest what might be learned from similar analyses in real cities."

The Commission also turned to a model to show how the frustrating and unfair delay between arrest and trial in the nation's overcrowded courts might be studied. The first job was to simulate the flow of 1550 cases through the District Court of the District of Columbia for the year 1965, where the process often took five months or more as compared to a recommended maximum of four months, and then to simulate possible ways of speeding the flow. A computer was programmed to reproduce the activities of the court according to a regular schedule of five days a week, allowing for holidays off and for closing at five in the afternoon.

The computer program for the first day incorporated the so-called Monte Carlo method, which in effect instructed the machine to pick a number at random between 20 and 80, representing the court's actual variation in daily number of cases. About 85 percent of these cases are released by the District Attorney. The rest are charged with one of four types of crime, are presented either to the General Sessions Court or to the United States Commissioner, and must then wait for various periods until being indicted. The entire process is a network of alternative procedures. There are about 50 to 60 points in the network where one of two or more different steps may be taken, and at each point the Monte Carlo technique determined possible outcome.

In other words, the computer was programmed to

reproduce what happened to District Court felony cases in 1965. Its validity was checked by providing it with the total number of cases for 1960 and 1955, and by noting that its statistical breakdown of how the cases were handled corresponded closely to actual records. Then the Commission studied effects of various changes on the system, and reported a finding that came as a surprise to many lawyers and judges —namely, that the total time from arrest to final trial could be reduced twenty-five percent by providing an extra grand jury part of the time. Furthermore, if this change were combined with others the time could be reduced from a median of five months to about three months.

The usual warning is in order. Models represent enormous simplifications of the real world, and a great deal more information and research are required before model results can be used to determine policy changes. As a matter of fact, the Commission also emphasized the lack of appropriate data and the need for a national information system which would include complete, up-to-date and readily accessible records. The need was dramatized in 1957 when investigators discovered a secret meeting of some seventy-five crime bosses in Apalachin, N. Y., and tried to obtain their full police records. The record of one criminal was scattered in more than two hundred police files, and two years later the records for all the criminals still had not been gathered.

The Commission's report has implications for educational problems. As far as the systems approach is concerned, simulation models have been used to study the flow of students through various courses and this work will be discussed in a later chapter. Not only that, but there is a particular relevance in the recommendation that systems research groups be established on a permanent staff basis in the larger criminal justice agencies. Disinterested outsiders can make significant contributions but, in the words of one veteran administrator, "Things really begin to happen when the drive comes from men within the organization—that's when the glacier becomes an avalanche."

## Social Problem Analysis

Things are beginning to move faster in all public areas. In health, for example, the United States ranks fifteenth among nations in its infant death rate—and a recent cost-effectiveness computer study shows that the best way to reduce this toll is to establish a $90 million birth-control program (which, incidentally, would be seven times more effective than the next most effective alternative, full maternal care). In the war against poverty the Office of Economic Opportunity has conducted similar studies including the already-mentioned Capsburg model and one of its findings also points out the importance of birth control, indicating that if family planning had been started a generation ago there would be about 4,500,-000 fewer poor people in the United States today.

In urban renewal and design the emphasis is on broader research. Most work to date has involved traffic and transportation which, as already indicated, include many situations that can be investigated by mathematical and engineering techniques. And yet, even in this relatively impersonal, mechanical aspect of city planning, social factors assume greater and greater significance the deeper one's analysis goes. Indeed, John Meyer at Harvard finds that racial factors lie at the root of many so-called transportation problems. Urban transportation systems are often well designed for white collar commuters who live in white suburbs but are very poorly designed for blue collar Negro workers who live in the city and must travel to jobs outside city limits. Meyer believes, "Some of those who talk about a transport crisis and want to see something done about it, may in reality just be asking, consciously or unconsciously, for more help in separating themselves from Negroes."

This illustrates a central fact about the entire urban situation. The city has become a kind of focal point where everything seems to come together, where all problems seem to find their most intense and most vivid expression. Water-resources problems often tend to be chiefly urban problems and the same thing goes for problems of crime, overcrowded courts, pollution, health and welfare, and civil rights. And, as will become evident in the rest of this book, many of the most urgent problems of education itself come to a head in a big-city setting.

# CHAPTER 5

# FOCUS ON EDUCATION

IN EDUCATION, as in other areas, the systems approach is evolving as part of the effort to achieve order and direction in the teeth of accelerating changes. We are moving so swiftly in the rapids of history that something strange seems to be happening to the future. There may have been a time, perhaps in the rosiest days of Victorian England, when the future had a remote and romantic quality, like land sighted far away from a sailing ship adrift in a calm sea. Notions about the shape of things to come made good conversation among gentlemen relaxing evenings in the drawing room or at the club.

Now the future is no longer remote. The last twenty years or so have brought it very close, first with radar and rockets and nuclear power, and more recently with spaceships and planned trips to the moon and Mars and beyond. And at the same time, although in less spectacular fashion perhaps, "science fiction" is also coming true in education. Education as a way, *the* way ultimately, to a better world—as a force against poverty, ill health, and crime—is less a utopian idea than it was a generation ago. We know that survival depends on it. Yesterday's long-run possibilities have suddenly become today's programs, because we really have no choice. In many cases the "long run" is a matter of a few years, and some people do not want to wait that long.

The pace of events has brought about a wider awareness of what education can contribute to welfare and economic and social development. In 1956, when the nation was spending some $17 billion a year on education, Vannevar Bush told a Congressional investigating committee that the Soviet Union was graduating engineers twice as fast as the United States, and technicians thirty to forty times as fast. That was the year before the launching of Sputnik I. Today the education budget is more than $65 billion, and a good chance exists that it may even exceed the defense budget in a few years.

This level of spending is one reason for the increased interest in the systems approach. Large sums of money are being earmarked for the extensive testing and development of innovations, and the problem of evaluating alternatives demands techniques and insights accumulated over the years by systems specialists. Also it is worth pointing out once more that we are less sure of ourselves than was once the case. Experiences with world wars, among other upheavals of the recent past, encourage educators and others concerned with the quality of future generations to search for new programs and plans and new ways of evaluating them.

## Measuring Effectiveness: Lowe and Taylor

There is a notable shift of emphasis when it comes to measuring effectiveness. The tendency is less to ask how well we, the educators, are doing. Not that efforts to assess educational systems are new, but earlier studies failed for a variety of political and administrative reasons, and also because they were oversold by enthusiasts who saw in them easy solutions to difficult problems. In 1862 Robert Lowe, vice president of Britain's Committee of the Privy Council for Education, introduced a "payment by results" plan for public elementary education. The plan stipulated that pupils' grades in the three R's should serve as criteria for the allocation of funds to individual schools. The intent was "to benefit the working classes . . . to insure that education be given to the poor just as much as to the rich."

Opposition was prompt and violent. A commentator summarized the reasons: "There was a kind of vague fear that the Church and Constitution were about to be undermined. . . . Mr. Lowe set against himself and his policy the country clergy, the official inspectors of schools, and the uncertificated schoolmasters. Here, they exclaimed with one voice, is a dreadful person; a man who actually demands to know for what reason he hands over to us the money of the nation." The plan failed in its original form and Lowe resigned two years later, after Parliament passed what he considered a no confidence vote.

Analogous problems arose somewhat later in the United States, largely because of too ready and uncritical an acceptance (rather than rejection) of measuring methods. The period from about 1910 to 1930 saw the "knowledge industry" notion carried to fantastic lengths in the name of better education. Frederick Taylor and other engineers pioneering in scientific management had developed methods of increasing the productivity of manufacturing plants, and numerous attempts were made to apply the methods wholesale to the running of public schools. The big theme was efficiency, and the big assumption was that what was good for American business was automatically good for American education.

Time-motion studies of men at machines inspired charts for rating teachers on the basis of time spent in passing out papers and other activities. The businessman's dread of idleness in general, and idle plant time in particular, was translated into the "platoon" system which made a fetish of efforts to schedule students so that all school rooms were being used all the time. In what amounted to a burlesque of cost-effectiveness analysis, one superintendent revealed that in his school system a dollar purchased 23.8 pupil recitations of French but only 5.9 pupil recitations of Greek—and stated that if the price of teaching Greek were not reduced, "We shall invest in something else."

On the other hand, there were some genuine insights in the midst of such absurdities. Scientific management had something to offer education, and many educators realized it. It recognized the fundamental importance of intensive research, of defining objectives, and of gathering and analyzing relevant information, although the task of data-processing might have proved prohibitively formidable in a precomputer era. Certainly the money required for this sort of work was not forthcoming. Education was expected to follow industry's lead without the funds industry spent routinely to improve its operations. In any case, the stress on emulating industry subsided somewhat as an aftermath of the Great Depression.

This attitude has by no means vanished. But it plays a less dominant role in today's thinking, a fortunate development considering the nature of the problems confronting us. A new kind of interest in the student himself is evolving, along with new efforts to measure the effectiveness of education. In a sense, until relatively recent times at least, the school was always right. Students capable of learning most of what it had to offer them were good students and candidates for higher education; other students were by definition less gifted and could go just so far and no further. In other words, the tendency was to emphasize student limitations, which is hardly a way of encouraging changes in the educational system.

Today the focus is more and more on positive factors, on differences rather than limitations. More and more attention is being paid to the unique combination of qualities which make the student an individual. Here also we have the power to do now or in the near future what was regarded not long ago as a remote possibility at best, namely to help the student develop and express himself in his own way. Of course, recognizing differences necessarily complicates matters. It means more of everything—more flexibility, more alternative courses, more evaluating, and a greater demand for the systems approach.

## Systems Analysis and the Coleman Report

So this demand represents a crucial part of new plans to increase educational opportunity. The sys-

tems approach is being used in a variety of different
ways and, roughly speaking, at three different levels:
1) in studies which involve the school systems of
entire cities or states, or the entire nation; 2) in
studies designed to understand the workings of individual institutions; and 3) in studies concentrating
primarily on individual courses and teaching methods.
It should be pointed out again that as far as education
and the public area in general are concerned, the
studies are all at early stages of development.

At the broadest or national level the major effort so
far has gone into what is known in the systems trade
as "establishing a firm data base." What this means
in terms of sheer work may be illustrated by one of
the largest statistical studies ever undertaken in the
field of education, the "Equality of Educational Opportunity" report, on which a group of investigators
and consultants spent a year and $1.5 million working
under the direction of James Coleman of Johns Hopkins University. A major objective was to spell out as
precisely as possible (in view of existing time limits)
the extent to which student achievement and school
quality were related to the student's family background and to such factors as the family's economic
and racial status.

The survey, which was supported by the U.S. Office
of Education, obtained information consisting of 300
to 400 items for each of more than 500,000 students in
some 6000 public schools throughout the nation. The
data were first broken down to indicate the relative
effects of various factors on achievement, and were
then subjected to a statistical technique known as
"regression analysis," which in effect isolates the
most sensitive factors—that is, those that make the

biggest differences. Of course, doing all the arithmetic required for these analyses would have been out of the question without the high-speed electronic computer; the fastest available computer took about 300 hours to perform calculations that would have required thousands of years using desk-type adding machines.

The Coleman report, reinforcing many smaller-scale reports, provides measures of the widening achievement gap between white and nonwhite students. For example, as far as reading comprehension in the metropolitan schools of the northeast United States is concerned, sixth-grade Negro students are nearly two years behind sixth-grade white students, and the gap increases to about three years by the twelfth grade. The report also has a great deal to say about the importance of the socioeconomic level of the student and of his classmates, student and parental attitudes toward education, vocational training, and so on.

But for all its 737 pages it is only a first step in a long-term research program, and a number of studies are under way to refine and extend its numerous findings. For example, Office of Education statisticians are working on a mathematical model which goes beyond the Coleman report and is making it possible to rank more precisely the effects of various factors on student learning, achievement, and choice of careers. The next step will involve maximizing techniques such as those used to determine the make-up of nursing staffs for hospital wards and the most effective combination of cultural activities in State Department overseas programs (see Chapters 3 and 4). In this case one aim will be to determine the best mixtures of conditions, the best allocations of educational and social resources, required to increase the achievement scores of various students with various social and economic backgrounds.

Another national model is being developed to investigate how students of different backgrounds do in colleges and universities. The model simulates the year-by-year histories of individual students, the grades they are likely to receive, the level of their general academic interest, the funds available to them, and so on. A major point of interest is the relationship of dropouts to the financial gap between college tuition fees and the amount of money the student's family can afford to pay. Joseph Froomkin, Assistant Commissioner for Program Planning and Evaluation, has been directly involved in the shaping of this and other models and emphasizes how much remains to be done: "We have a long way to go in our attempts to respond effectively to the crisis in education. But not long ago our cupboard was bare of good evaluation studies, and this is no longer the case today."

## National Assessment

This work represents one phase of the drive to obtain information about the effects of current policies and practices. In 1964 the Carnegie Corporation launched a "National Assessment of Educational Progress" program, a kind of national poll or census of what people have learned. The poll is still in the planning stage and will involve the questioning of population samples made up of 256 groups subdivided into the following categories—boys and girls, four geographic regions (Northeast, South, Midwest, Far

West), four age groups (nine, thirteen, seventeen, and thirty), four social environments (large city, small city, suburban, rural), and two economic levels.

Questionnaires, interviews and other techniques will be used to assess reading and writing skills as well as knowledge and skills in sciences, mathematics, social studies, citizenship, art, music, literature, and the vocational areas. The general idea is to repeat the poll at regular intervals of three to five years, analyze significant changes, and relate the changes both to the effectiveness of past educational procedures and to the design of future procedures. This project and those under way at the Office of Education are essentially pioneering efforts, necessary preliminary steps toward obtaining the data which will serve as the basis for more and more sophisticated models and other systems techniques.

## School Planning in Sweden

It should be noted that the increasing use of the systems approach in education is an international development. One of the most striking examples of the trend may be found in Sweden where the educational system has been completely reconstructed during the past generation. For one thing compulsory education has been extended from seven to nine years, and provisions have been made to encourage further school attendance on a voluntary basis. Students entering the ninth grade may choose one of nine different "streams" or types of curriculum which emphasize either the theoretical or practical aspects of liberal arts, social studies, and the sciences—and which prepare the way for related work at upper secondary and higher levels.

As a result, upper secondary education is no longer the "socially exclusive" system it was in 1946 when only eight percent of Sweden's sixteen-year-olds were admitted. The present level is more than thirty percent, and college and university enrollments have increased by about the same proportion. Although changes in the Swedish educational system have, to date, been based largely on straightforward fact-finding and projections, systems research, used selectively and strategically, has had a major effect on parliamentary decisions. Studies of the relationship between achievement and social class—resembling certain work presented in the Coleman report—helped overcome widespread prejudices against making higher education available to a greater proportion of young people.

Future plans include wider use of mathematical models already worked out to investigate teacher supply-and-demand problems and the comprehensive operations of schools and universities. (These and other studies await the gathering of further data.) The systems approach is regarded as especially important in view of the avowed policy of "rolling" or constant reform. According to a recent report, "Swedish authorities do not regard the series of reforms adopted in various sectors of the educational system as fixed for any period, but rather see them as being subject to continuing trial and experimentation."

## OECD Educational Planning

Work in Sweden and elsewhere has been supported by the OECD or Organization for Economic Cooperation and Development. This international agency, which was established in 1961 by the United States and some twenty European nations, exists among

other things "to achieve the highest sustainable economic growth and employment and a rising standard of
living in member nations." Its interest in the systems
approach is an outgrowth of a program which it has
sponsored in six Mediterranean countries (Greece,
Italy, Portugal, Spain, Turkey, Yugoslavia) and which
ties long-range educational plans directly to forecasts
of manpower requirements based on estimates of expected economic growth.

The extent of overseas commitments to the systems
approach is indicated in the proceedings of a three-
day OECD meeting held recently in Paris and devoted exclusively to the role of systems techniques in
educational planning. Discussions covered a wide
range of subjects, from models designed to investigate
possible ways of reducing teacher shortages in British
secondary schools to a German model for estimating
how much of his life an individual might best allocate
to full-time study, part-time study, and full-time work.
Another maximizing model, dealing with the entire
French economy and supported by the French Planning Commission, is concerned with the best way of
allocating national resources between industrial and
educational developments.

These are tentative, exploratory models. Every
model is by definition a simplification of some real-life
situation, but the basic question is how much of a
simplification. The gap between most educational models being developed today and the actual conditions
they are designed to examine is still too great to
permit the translation of model results into direct
action. But the results often indicate trends, suggest
new policies, or lend support to policies already being
followed. For example Samuel Bowles, a Harvard

economist who spent two years as a civil servant in the educational system of Northern Nigeria, has used an allocation-of-resources model to explore the implications of some of that region's current policies.

## Nigerian and Greek Models

Dr. Bowles found that the model offered important new insights many of which contradict intuitions based on his field experience and, incidentally, happen to support the policies if not necessarily the logic of certain Nigerian politicians. He started out with the feeling that primary education was tremendously expensive relative to the associated benefits and that too much money was being spent on it, money that might be better spent on secondary and technical education. But analysis with the aid of the model indicates the advisability for the immediate future not only of a rapid expansion in primary education but a reduction in secondary and technical enrollments. It turns out that, although economic benefits from primary education are not high, the costs are even lower, so that net gains are impressive. "This is the sort of course that is politically popular," Bowles comments, "because more primary education is just what the people want."

Other analyses concern teacher training, the effects of a proposed government policy to reduce primary education from seven to five years without reducing total classroom hours (a ten percent net increase in estimated economic benefits), and the optimum number of foreign teachers to import considering the trade-off between the benefits of more rapid educational expansion and welfare losses resulting from increased dependence on foreigners (about 2700). The Nigerian government is not at present making use of the model.

But Bowles has recently applied his model to the Greek educational system and economy, and another economist has used it in analyzing resource allocation in Canadian education.

Meanwhile planning proceeds in the United States at state and municipal as well as national levels. Since space does not permit a comprehensive account of studies being conducted under the auspices of various state departments of education, we shall present only a few examples to indicate the scope of some major projects. The projects are of interest not only in themselves but also because they illustrate the dangers of overselling the systems approach and indicate why spectacular improvements are not to be expected in a hurry. Progress in all cases depends to a large extent on that phase of the systems approach which involves developing a model and collecting relevant data.

## New York State Planning

As emphasized in Chapter 2, a central problem is to establish measurements which will tell us where we stand and where we are heading in our efforts to attain specified goals. One of the most important studies along these lines has just begun in close collaboration between the New York State Education Department and Educational Testing Service. In the fall of 1966 at a New York conference of the Educational Records Bureau, Norman Kurland, director of the Department's Center on Innovation suggested that work be done on a type of measurement new to educators but long familiar to economists:

Techniques have been developed which make it possible to compare data from year to year and from one part of the (economic) system to another. They are presented so that one can get a reading on the entire economy as with the indicator on the Gross National Product, or one can go behind this to the many indicators that are combined to make up the GNP. . . . Thus the average citizen can derive some meaning from the Cost of Living Index, a busy executive can relate his decisions to the Wholesale Price Index. . . . As we contemplate committing greatly increased resources to education, we ought to be able to determine whether one use is any better than another. If we do not we shall swing from fad to fad, ever changing and never improving.

Kurland called for the development of educational performance indicators, and research toward that end is proceeding at Educational Testing Service on the basis of a so-called "student-change" model. The model takes into consideration the effect of the total educational process—the impact of school, home, and community—on students at various stages during their school careers. The result will not be a single measure of how the educational system is performing, but "a matrix of performance measures"—a set of indicators showing how students at different grade or age levels are changing with respect to reading skill and other aspects of cognitive development, physical condition, interpersonal behavior, and so on.

The indicators by their very nature will be estimates rather than highly precise measures of performance, but estimates which educators will be able to use in arriving at decisions about where to concentrate their efforts. Specific steps and plans, of course, will depend on evaluations of teaching techniques and innovations available to those responsible for improving the educational system. According to a recent report, the indicators are expected to play a role in "reducing to some extent the guesswork in allocating resources and deploying educational personnel so as to maximize the effectiveness of the system."

Such work is being coordinated with other changes which draw heavily on the systems approach and require further data-gathering and evaluation. The State Budget Office, for example, is using cost-effectiveness analyses and program budgeting to justify appropriations for education as well as for other activities; and program-budgeting procedures being established by financial officers of the State University of New York will include detailed planning for the next ten to fifteen years. Furthermore, a computer system is under development which will eventually furnish predictions of college and university student enrollments at each of the state's 230 public and private campuses.

## Capsburg and Educating the Disadvantaged

The Capsburg U.S.A. model mentioned in Chapter I provides another interesting example of state activity. This model of a typical American city was designed by scientists at Philco's Operations Research and Long Range Planning Department for the Office of Economic Opportunity, as part of the war against poverty. It is now being revised as part of a major study being conducted by the Colorado State Department of Education. The model's original purpose was to help investigate the effectiveness of neighborhood health and service centers, legal aid, housing rehabilitation, and other community action programs. Such programs are exceedingly difficult to evaluate because they involve very slow changes in conditions and habits that have been established for generations.

The model was based on information obtained in the field survey of community action agencies in Atlanta, Newark, Philadelphia, Pittsburgh, Milwaukee, New Haven, and San Francisco and Oakland. It made use of available records and individual judgments having to do with the values of a variety of different projects. Punch-card instructions to a computer specified the probable long-range effects of each project on the earned income of families in poverty areas, their educational status, migratory patterns, and so on. The general aim was to predict the mixture of projects which would yield the highest return per dollar spent.

One trial computer run, for example, investigated a program costing $775,000 a year and made up of seven projects. Four of the projects (small business development, Head Start preschool sessions, remedial education in elementary school, dropout counseling in high schools) involved the entire city of Capsburg. The three remaining projects (job development, year-round preschool training, work–study training) were carried out in the central nonwhite slum area only. The computer simulated social and economic changes in the city over a period of sixteen years, from 1966 to 1982, calculating the results for each two-year period in about thirty seconds, which represents a speed-up factor of more than a million.

Part of the simulation concerned educational status, and here changes with and without the program were compared. The rising demand for job applicants with at least a high school education seems to be a sufficiently important factor to produce some effect in the absence of any community action project at all. During the first two years of the "no program" computer run, the proportion of Capsburg citizens with only one to seven years of education dropped from 45 to about 38 percent. But after that there was little change; the proportion tended to remain at that level for the remaining fourteen years.

The antipoverty program made little difference for the first ten years of the run, but between 1976 and 1978 it produced a sharp drop in this undereducated segment of the population, from about 37 to 22 percent. During the entire sixteen-year period the program reduced the number of nonwhites earning less than $3000 a year from 45 to about 21 percent. It is interesting to note that in such runs certain projects were dropped in the computer simulation because they did not seem to be working out, while others were retained even though they did not produce results for a decade or more. Also, despite all the improvements, the central nonwhite slum area remained a slum for the period of the simulation. People moved out as they earned more money, but their places were taken by low-income people moving in from surrounding rural areas.

These trial runs were indicative only. Most of the results appeared reasonable as far as the best available judgments were concerned and probably provided a good idea of basic trends. But the art of developing models demands constant feedback, constant testing and adjusting on the basis of new data, and retesting and re-adjusting. The Capsburg model was first tested with real data in New Haven during the summer of 1966, by starting with 1960 statistics on family income, employment, and other factors and "predicting" known

1962 statistics. It is accurately being refined as a tool in antipoverty research.

The Colorado Department of Education project involves a greatly expanded version of the model. Capsburg has become Denver with its five surrounding counties and at least thirty areas and a population of more than 1,200,000 persons. The Department's Division of Urban Education has been gathering data required for a series of computer runs which will furnish preliminary predictions of how various educational changes will affect the economic and social growth of metropolitan Denver, and particularly the social and economic advancement of minority groups.

## PACE in California

Still considering activities at the statewide level, one of the most ambitious and elaborate complexes of plans is unfolding in California. The plans are based in part on studies of the California State Department of Education by the Arthur D. Little consulting firm in Cambridge, Massachusetts, One development, known as Projects to Advance Creativity in Education, or PACE for short, involves twenty-odd centers distributed throughout the state to establish priorities among existing educational problems and submit proposals for solutions. According to an educator associated with the centers, "They have already been helpful in getting the counties to communicate, cooperate and think on a larger scale."

A unique phase of the program is a project aimed at what is undoubtedly one of the most serious problems in advanced educational planning wherever it is attempted—the critical shortage not only of systems specialists, but also of people familiar enough with the workings and potentialities of the systems approach to seek out the specialists for the work that has to be done. The California project is designed to teach educators and administrators the broad principles of the approach, so that they will eventually be able to play an active and constructive role in various organizations such as the PACE centers. Current intentions are to train some 5000 persons by 1970.

## New England Assessment

Trained administrators and systems specialists are also needed in broad-gauge regional programs financed by the Office of Education and calling for the cooperation of the departments of education of several states. One such program, the New England Educational Assessment Project, has been organized to provide "vital statistical information and data collection techniques necessary for the development of improved educational programs" in the elementary and secondary schools of the region. It includes studies of the role of teacher aides, the reading achievements of third-grade pupils, and improved counseling systems—and as time passes it is sure to turn more and more to program budgeting along with model building and other ways of evaluating benefits offered by alternative plans.

Finally, a number of studies have been organized under local auspices by local educators and administrators concerned in the main with improvements within urban and suburban communities. Such studies are particularly significant in counteracting a tendency which has been noted in another area and may apply to education as well. In a recent report Daniel Moynihan, head of the Harvard–M.I.T. Joint Center for

Urban Studies, summarized the problem as follows:
"The United States has quite possibly the best employment data in the world, but there is not a city in the nation that knows what its unemployment rate is."

## Cleveland Yardstick Project

Nationwide and statewide studies are obviously of enormous importance, but sooner or later everything boils down to action in school districts and schools. An example of work at the local level is the so-called "Yardstick Project" in Cleveland. The emphasis here is on doing something within three years, and within a budget of $275,000 provided by Cleveland's Jennings Foundation. The project is notable for relying strongly on the systems approach from the very beginning, for building the approach into its planning. According to its director Fred Pinkham, "Our goal is to find ways of helping school boards and school administrators develop realistic levels of expectation in performance, measure progress toward their objectives, and create a flow of information in a form useful to them in their planning and policy-making."

A study has been made of the records of several hundred students from a number of graduating classes in four suburban school systems in the Cleveland area. The study has been carried out under the direction of the systems specialist Leonard Arnoff of the accountant firm of Ernst & Ernst, and has involved other consultants including Burton Dean of the School of Management at Case Western Reserve University and Thomas James of Stanford University. It required a detailed statistical analysis of the students' interests, achievements, social and economic backgrounds, test scores, and so on—as well as community characteristics, school organization, teachers, curriculum, and finance.

The major outcome has been a new and more complete picture of educational potentials and expectations, an index to what might be accomplished given the particular communities and pupils, and current school conditions. The analysis has succeeded in identifying some of the factors in the records which help to indicate how well a pupil is doing with respect to his potentialities and also help to predict his future performance in school and college. Eventually each school system will record its own data, carry out its own computations, and chart its own results.

Another phase of the Yardstick Project is the development of a computer model to investigate the operation of a local school system or any part thereof. The model, like the Capsburg model, will provide a high-speed history of simulated events—in this case, of expected increases in enrollment and expected demands for more teachers, funds, and space. It will then be possible to evaluate how various contemplated changes in educational policies and practices may affect the course of these events. (A somewhat more detailed discussion of the workings of such models is presented in the following chapter.)

## Quincy and Philadelphia

Two further simulation models are of interest in connection with educational planning at the city level. One of them was developed in 1966 for the Quincy (Mass.) School Committee by Arthur D. Little analysts to predict 1970 enrollments in all the city's schools from kindergarten through the twelfth grade. The predictions were used to specify the number and nature of new schools as well as construction schedules and architectural details; and current plans are proceeding according to these recommendations. Also, a model of the entire School District of Philadelphia is being developed by Roger Sisson of the University of Pennsylvania, with the cooperation of David Horowitz and his associates at the District's Office of Planning.

The examples of systems studies presented in this chapter are of interest as indications of the use of scientific, functional planning in education. But even more important, they serve to direct attention to the nature of the forces which are influencing the educational process. Civic pride, efforts to attack the fundamental causes of crime and poverty, considerations of national power and economic growth, the desire to achieve equal opportunity among peoples here and now and not in some remote utopian future—all these pressures are coming into play to a greater extent than ever before, and all at once. It is hardly surprising that the repercussions are being felt increasingly in state and federal agencies.

# CHAPTER 6

# UNIVERSITY RESEARCH

## CAMPUS GAME

*Simulation Examples—Case 2*

*Variable is New Student Enrollment: 600*

THIS CAPTION, appearing in a university of Toronto research paper published in 1966, introduces a study of the department of science and the department of liberal arts in a hypothetical university. The "game" was played on a computer programmed to answer the following question: What changes in space, staff, and cost would be required for the academic year if 600 new students enrolled instead of the expected 500?

The computer, carrying out its prepared instructions, presented answers in the form of a tabulated "print-out." The twenty-percent increase in enrollment would call for a total of 56,940 extra square feet of classroom and office space for the two departments (increasing the percent of available space utilized from 60 to 67.5), six extra teachers (four assistant professors and two full professors), and an additional administrative clerk. The additional cost would be $95,040. To arrive at such figures the computer spent a fraction of a second automatically analyzing data on the distribution of students in various courses within the departments, class size, number of weekly meetings, and so on.

Two further computer games were played to explore ways of handling the additional students. What would be the effect on staff and budget if the teaching load were increased by an average of two hours in each department? (Five fewer full professors, seven fewer assistant professors, two fewer administrative clerks, and a cost reduction of $173,200.) What would it cost to double administrative support under such conditions? ($45,100.) Other games indicated the results of increasing academic salaries, adding a science course to the liberal arts program, and so on. The paper emphasized that the simulation model was presented for demonstration purposes only—that "certain liberties have been taken with reality for the sake of simplicity."

But the model represented an early step toward a far more realistic model recently completed by one of the very few and one of the most successful organizations of its kind, the University of Toronto's Office of Institutional Research. The Office is unusual for a number of reasons. For one thing, it is a systems organization and exists exclusively to apply the systems approach to university problems. Its professional staff consists of Director Bertrand Hansen, a systems specialist from Ohio State University where he developed simulation models for the Air Force, and for young associates. (The "senior" associate is 28 years old.) They operate on a total annual budget of about

$80,000, or less than one eighth of one percent of the university budget.

The establishment of the Office can be traced to a 1965 report by Richard Judy, Professor of Economics and Computer Science, and Jack Levine, a graduate student working for his doctor's degree in systems research. The report, *A New Tool For Educational Administrators*, was among other things a first-rate introduction to the systems approach. It emphasized the importance of defining objectives and obtaining the information necessary to back up major decisions, and the danger of making such decisions solely by intuition: "Information deficiency means excess capacity here and shortages there; it means unsubstantiated budgets; it means emergency appeals for funds; it means that the educational investment is not paying its maximum dividend."

## The CAMPUS Model

The report also spelled out some of the basic principles of model building, presenting a pilot simulation model known as CAMPUS (Comprehensive Analytical Model for Planning in the University Sphere). It included sample computer print-outs, graphs indicating the sort of ten-year projections that could be obtained for future budget and staff requirements, and examples of the technique of investigating policies "on the simulation model before they are implemented." Furthermore the report was an excellent job of salesmanship and, together with Professor Judy's persuasive in-person arguments, played a leading role in convincing administrative officials of the value of a special systems office.

Dr. Hansen arrived in Toronto in July 1966, his

main task being to gather data for a large-scale CAMPUS model of the entire university. But the systems approach proved itself in several cases even before the model was developed, mainly because of evidence gathered in the course of preparatory studies. For example Hansen's first major problem arose less than two months after he started work. It came in the form of an announcement by the Provincial Government of Ontario.

As a result of careful studies of its educational requirements, the government decided to institute a new policy of using "formula financing" for its fourteen universities that receive public support, a scheme which bases funding of operating requirements on total enrollments and the weighted costs of training students in forty-two different fields or categories. (For example, the cost of a Ph.D. education is represented by a weight of 6, as compared with 3 for a degree in medicine or law, 2 for an undergraduate degree in engineering or architecture, and 1 for an undergraduate degree in general science or liberal arts.

Judy and Hansen and their associates built a computer model in a hurry to gauge the impact of this policy. It took them five days to prepare instructions which enabled a computer to carry out a retrospective analysis—to examine data from the past three academic years on the number of students in each category at all fourteen universities, proposed weightings, and income received from all sources. The analysis indicated that while the University of Toronto was still receiving the lion's share of provincial funds, the lion's share was beginning to get smaller because other universities were growing at a faster rate. Another finding was that if formula financing had been in effect during the past three years the University of Toronto would have received from 12 to about 20 percent more money from the provincial government than it actually received.

Looking forward, however, indicated somewhat less favorable trends. For 1967–68, the first year of formula financing, all Ontario universities actually received about ten percent less support than had been expected on the basis of computer-prepared projections. The difference came to about $6 million for the University of Toronto, an amount much greater than it should have been, and a check-up revealed a discrepancy involving differing opinions about the relative importance of graduate studies and the proper weighted costs for certain courses of study. The special value of having undertaken model studies, from both university and government standpoints, quickly became evident at this stage. Because the model provided a way of obtaining solid data relevant specifically to the point at issue, university officials were ready to argue their case more cogently, and representatives of the provincial government were ready to listen.

The outcome of a series of meetings, and a statement justifying the university's case, was a compromise. The university recovered one-third of the discrepancy, a total of about $2 million in additional grants. And, what was even more significant in relation to long-term policy, its advisory committee on the operating budget had a firm quantitative basis for planning in accordance with the new situation. In other words, it knew in fairly concrete terms the trade-offs involved and the results of suggested economies. For example, the final adjustment meant hiring fewer new professors, and one result was continuing at the current student-teacher ratio of 13.5 instead of lowering the ratio to about 12.5.

## CAMPUS and Information Retrieval

Continuing work on the CAMPUS model has had other results. The model requires considerable data for the past as well as the present and future, material contained in the university's operating budgets from 1952 on. But these budgets were conventional budgets which, as pointed out earlier, include general categories like maintenance, salaries, and so on—and as a rule provide little information about plans and objectives. On the other hand, analytical techniques make it possible to get at relevant information buried among the categories, and Hansen and his associates used such techniques to extract the data and put them on punchcards for computer studies.

A series of more than twenty summary reports made the information available for the first time in readily accessible form, and has brought about a widening re-examination of various long-standing practices. New facts obtained from the old budgets, facts pertaining to salary policies and other intradepartmental matters have encouraged a number of departments to undertake more intensive surveys of their own operations. In a sort of chain reaction a questionnaire developed by Hansen's group led the Department of Political Economy to prepare a still more detailed questionnaire, which has in turn led to similar work in other departments.

In general, model building has helped to open up new lines of communication within and among departments, as well as to accelerate quantitative studies of many kinds. For example, a preliminary step in determining overall space requirements was to make an inventory of all laboratories, offices, lecture halls, and so on—and then to find out what proportion of the space was actually being used at any given time, applying research methods developed by investigators at the University of Wisconsin and Purdue University. Plans are currently being developed to increase the efficiency of space utilization from about fifty to more than seventy percent.

The completed CAMPUS model represents two years of work, and will undoubtedly serve as a prototype for models to be developed in the future at other educational institutions. In concrete form it consists of a set of instructions coded on 3000 punchcards; instructions which cause the computer to process some 500,000 items of information describing the university for every year to be simulated. During a simulation the machine analyzes the flow of 25,000 full-time and part-time students through some fifty departments offering about two hundred different academic programs toward undergraduate and graduate degrees. (The only part of the university not included in the model is the medical school which will double in size by 1971 and has a special seven-man systems staff and a budget of $300,000 to help it prepare for the rapid expansion.)

The computer model may be regarded as a system made up of four sections involving enrollments, resources, budget, and space. Information flows from one section to another according to rules specified in the programmed instructions. The basic input data, facts about the structure of the university and the number of students expected, are translated into departmental work loads in the model's enrollment section. The work-load information, together with further information about teaching load and about class size and composition, then flows into the resources section which computes staff and general space requirements for each department. This information in turn passes to the budget and space sections and is processed to yield essential output data concerning academic costs, administrative costs, general expenses, and academic and administrative space requirements.

## Program Budgeting with CAMPUS

Predictions based on expected enrollments can be made for periods up to ten years in the future, at an average computing speed of about two minutes for each year. The first major project, currently under way, involves a five-year projection and is especially significant because it illustrates the evolution of the systems approach in a university setting. The process of developing a model, of identifying controllable and uncontrollable variables and constraints, inevitably directs attention to objectives and ways of carrying them out. As a result, the data gathered become more and more oriented toward objectives and programs, so the trend is to orient budgetary procedures accordingly. In this sense, model building prepares the way for program budgeting.

That is what has happened at the University of Toronto. Even before the completion of the CAMPUS model, program budgeting was introduced throughout the university as a natural development of the systems approach. Furthermore, the next step of the process is already being carried out. Just as model building and data gathering may lead to program budgeting, so program budgeting itself leads directly to associated techniques devised to help administrators achieve an optimum allocation of resources—namely, the techniques of "constrained maximization" which has played and is still playing an enormously important role in the application of the systems approach to a variety of military, industrial, and governmental problems (see Chapter 3).

This outstanding record may be traced to an unusual combination of circumstances. The basic impetus came from the political arena in the form of increased funds for education. For the single academic year 1966–67 to 1967–68 the contributions of the provincial government of Ontario to university operating budgets have risen by about fifty percent, which probably represents the highest rate of increase on the American continent. So everything is especially intense and urgent at the present time—the emphasis on research and innovation, and also the competition as each university makes its case for a share of available funds.

Under such conditions the University of Toronto is in a position to take the lead in systems studies. It has the facilities, including a large faculty and a large general-purpose computer. It also happens to have a climate in which the systems approach can flourish: what one observer has referred to as "a very progressive top administration which actually responds to the recommendations of its committees." The organizational status of the Office of Institutional Research reflects this situation. It is built into the university at the highest administrative level and operates on university funds rather than uncertain grants from the outside. Hansen, as Special Assistant to the President and also as director of the Office, has access to all information and sits in on all policy-shaping meetings.

Another important point involves communications between the Office and the rest of the university. Hansen has made a special effort to speak and write in uncluttered English, a sound and strategical policy judging by certain unfortunate experiences elsewhere. Every field of research develops its own jargon and the systems field is no exception, all of which may be relatively harmless as long as specialists confine their communications to one another. But the use of jargon in material prepared for administrators and other laymen is an effective way of losing one's audience, and one's support, and has accounted in large part for the bogging down of a number of technically valid projects.

Summarizing the state of affairs to date, the systems approach has first of all provided a store of quantitative information, a most substantial data base for continuing investigations. (One questionnaire alone involved about seventy different questions and was filled out by more than 800 faculty members.) In two years it has evolved to a stage where program budgeting and associated techniques are being used to obtain deeper and deeper insights into the workings of the university as an organic system—and into the logic of its present and proposed activities. As far as the outside world is concerned the approach represents a kind of long-distance early-warning device, an alerting mechanism which senses social and political developments when they are just beginning to emerge and permits the administration to plan and act accordingly.

## Charles Hitch and Planning at Berkeley

The Toronto story has been presented in some detail as a good example of the sort of coordinated effort required to produce results. Such examples are still rare, but the evidence indicates that they will become increasingly common during the next few years. The familiar pattern of events has already been unfolding at a few other pioneering institutions. For instance, many of the same techniques are being applied more and more extensively at the University of California, where the President is Charles Hitch, who originally brought the systems approach to the Department of Defense and was thus indirectly responsible for its subsequent spread inside and outside federal agencies.

Systems analysis for the University's nine campuses and 95,000 students is centered at the Office of Analytical Studies in Berkeley. It is headed by John Keller, who worked with Hitch in the Department of Defense, and has a staff of eight administrative specialists and three to six graduate students. During the past few years its outstanding record has been marked by the same sort of evolution that has taken place in Toronto. Although data gathering is never finished, a major project has been the preparation of a comprehensive prototype handbook of operating statistics for the entire university.

Model building has also reached an advanced stage. The original inspiration came in 1965 when Keller read the Judy–Levine report on a CAMPUS model for the University of Toronto, and within five months he and a graduate student, George Weathersby, had designed preliminary "cost simulation" models for the

Berkeley and Los Angeles campuses. At present there are a total of eight models, eight sets of punchcards, representing the university's eight general campuses (at Davis, Irvine, Riverside, San Diego, Santa Barbara, and Santa Cruz as well as Berkeley and Los Angeles).

Some of the most penetrating studies have been conducted on the Berkeley model. The Berkeley campus has gone on a year-round, four-quarter schedule with classes being offered during a three-month summer quarter, a move which is also scheduled to go into effect at the other campuses—and which introduces some intriguing problems for systems analysts. One reason for the extended year is to achieve an increased utilization of facilities, which results in appreciable capital-cost savings. On the other hand, a price must be paid in this case, because the summer is "nonpremium" time which means that students are reluctant to enroll during traditional vacation months, classes tend to be smaller, and instructional costs rise (since practically the same maintenance and teaching costs are involved for the smaller classes).

So Keller and his associates decided to use the computer model for a "break even" analysis. Their objective was to find out how far they could reduce the mean class size to reach the point where the increased operating costs would just equal the capital cost savings (all discounted to present values) due to more efficient use of facilities. The answer came out to about 20 to 25 percent. That is, losses and gains tended to balance out if classes which ordinarily range in size from 20 to 40 students in winter months drop to 15 to 30 students for the summer.

This percentage is not something hard and fast, of

course. But it serves as a valuable guide for administrators. It tells them that they have a reasonable latitude in offering courses for such nonpremium time as the summer quarters. (A similar kind of analysis can be used to plan classes for late afternoons and Saturdays during regular terms.) Specifically it means that although planners cannot offer a full range of courses, which might produce an uneconomical drop of 40 per cent in class size, they do not have to go to the other extreme and confine their offerings to only a relatively few highly popular courses. In other words, the summer sessions can include a more varied "menu" than might have been expected in the absence of model studies.

## The Berkeley Model and Reagan Budget Cuts

Another series of analyses concerned budget difficulties which arose during the spring of 1967 when California began an economy drive under Governor Ronald Reagan. As a general rule university planners are accustomed to dealing with moderate budget cuts in the ten-percent range by the usual process of cutting a bit here and trimming there. But the Reagan administration was speaking in terms of a cut of nearly 30 percent in state funds, a cut from $278 million to $197 million; and in the words of one commentator, "It is hard for traditional budgeteers to contemplate reductions of such magnitude."

The Berkeley computer model made it possible to examine the effects of a number of unusual budget-reducing procedures. For example, what would be the effect of stipulating that no graduate classes should have fewer than five students, that no undergraduate classes should have fewer than ten students

—but that in no case would the university tolerate an increase in mean class size of more than twenty percent (to prevent the wholesale elimination of small classes)? According to computer calculations, this set of constraints would produce an annual budget reduction of about $12 million. Further analyses estimated the savings that would result from increasing teaching loads, and from limiting undergraduate and graduate enrollments in various ways for different programs.

A current problem involves plans to increase the efficiency of graduate education. The demand for advanced degrees has risen rapidly during the past decade, but recent studies reveal a very high dropout rate at the University of California and at other comparable institutions. Indeed, indications are that for every 100 graduate students entering in the fall of one year, more than 40 will have left by the fall of the following year. Cost-simulation models are being used to estimate the effects of various countermeasures, such as more intensive interviews before students are admitted, more intensive counseling after admission, special courses to correct deficiencies in advanced mathematics or foreign languages, and so on.

Once these individual alternatives have been evaluated the next step is to find that mix of alternatives which will reduce graduate-student dropouts most for a given budget. "Downstream attrition"—dropouts occurring later in graduate education—is also a matter of concern, and tests will be conducted to evaluate the effects of increasing scholarship aid, providing a typing pool to assist students, and other corrective steps. Incidentally, a surprising discovery is that traditional notions about the costs of different graduate programs do not necessarily hold, if you allow for dropout rates and associated expenses. To cite one example, engineering, usually considered a high-cost program, is actually among the cheapest programs on the basis of the total cost per degree awarded—while programs in the humanities turn out to be fairly expensive.

About half a dozen other investigations are being carried out at the Office of Analytical Studies, including a projection of estimated enrollments and costs to the year 2000. Such developments are part of a broad policy to bring the use of models and the systems approach in general into university programs at all levels—not as something remote to be handled in a special computer center by experts only, but as a routine operation which educators may undertake whenever the impact of new administrative proposals is to be explored. In other words, the aim is to estimate the economic consequences of those proposals as simply, rapidly, and precisely as possible so that planners can choose more effectively among alternatives.

The first steps toward this end are already being taken. For instance if the chairman of a science department has a plan or several alternatives for increasing student participation in classroom demonstrations, there is a procedure for translating his ideas rapidly into terms of what they will cost and what allocations of resources will be required. First he fills out a recently developed questionnaire using ordinary conversational English. Then the information is transferred to punchcards, translated automatically into computer language, and used to prepare appropriate analyses. Keller expresses the general objective as follows: "Our goal is to achieve a dialogue between fiscal and academic planners, so that the academic planners will have the information they need to make judgments about the relative desirability of various academic programs."

## Case Western Reserve Planning

Some interesting developments are also taking place at Case Western Reserve University in Cleveland, the result of a recent merger of Western Reserve and the Case Institute of Technology. In 1951 one of the nation's earliest systems research groups was established at Case, which became an internationally known center for theoretical and applied studies in the field, and this tradition may influence future trends in administrative planning at the newly formed university. Progress is being made in the development of an imaginative program to train research specialists in education.

For several years Vernon Mickelson, director of the Case Office of Institute Planning, has been gathering information and working toward systems programs like those being conducted in Toronto and Berkeley. He has prepared an annual projection of expected enrollments, income, faculty and space requirements, costs, and other factors through the academic year 1975-76, and plans a major review of the projection every three years. Studies initiated in the Office identified and directed attention to the problem of attrition rates among freshmen entering Case, and indicated the need for moves to lighten study loads. These moves and other developments have reduced the proportion of pregraduation dropouts from 42 to less than thirty percent.

Another step toward a broad systems approach has

been taken in a 333-page doctoral thesis written by a graduate student, Caroline Boyer, with the cooperation of administrative officials and the School of Management faculty. The thesis, entitled *A Model of a Technical Education System,* is an intensive statistical analysis of the Case student body before the merger with Western Reserve. It presents a comprehensive report of overall university objectives, selection standards, performance tests, how freshmen use their time, the relationship between grades and achievement after graduation, the educational background of students' parents, and many other factors. The final chapter includes flow charts indicating what happens to undergraduate and graduate students after admission, charts that can serve as the basis for more detailed studies and computer models.

A most important development for the future of the systems approach is a new program which, in the words of Burton Dean of the School of Management, has been designed "to produce a new breed of investigator in education." The three-year program, supported by the Office of Education, trains selected graduate students to conduct research on key urban educational problems. One of its unique features involves courses in systems techniques expected to be especially useful in analyzing such problems, including techniques for solving assignment and scheduling problems like those described in Chapter 3.

The program has resulted in a number of projects which are to be completed next year. One student has made a survey of some fifty counselors and counseling assistants in the Cleveland area, as part of studies to document the wide difference between theory and practice—between what counselors are supposed to do and what they actually do. The survey indicates that a high-school student receives only about fifteen minutes of counseling per semester, and this finding is being followed by an allocation-of-resources analysis which will indicate those duties which best match the counselor's professional training and personality. Another student has been using data gathered in the Yardstick Project (see Chapter 5) in a similar analysis of how student performance in high school is related to college performance. Such training programs are particularly significant in view of the serious shortage of educators skilled in the systems approach.

The plans discussed in this chapter may be at different stages and may differ somewhat in emphasis, but they suggest some of the basic problems and activities associated with the use of the systems approach in the university environment. Work related to that being done in Toronto and Berkeley and Cleveland is also under way at Yale, Ohio State, Michigan State, Indiana, Penn State, Johns Hopkins, and a few other universities. The trend is toward more disciplined ways of evaluating, toward model building, intensive gathering of data, and the weighing of alternatives as a matter of routine. Faced with a variety of new problems and complexities, academic and fiscal planners are beginning to know their institutions in a new and deeper way.

# CHAPTER 7

# SYSTEMS IN THE SCHOOLS

IN ELEMENTARY and secondary schools, significant changes are under way which in effect are preparing for a greatly accelerated use of the systems approach. But a broad pattern of evolution has yet to emerge at this stage of the process. In many respects the situation seems to be more complicated than at the college and university levels. There are more problems associated with neighborhood and community relations and local politics, more alternatives to evaluate, and perhaps an even greater gap between what exists today and what we are striving to achieve tomorrow.

Certain developments have already been presented in Chapter 5. The Coleman report which documents factors in student achievement, the National Assessment of Educational Progress program to provide a census of current knowledge, the joint New York State Education Department–Educational Testing Service study involving performance indicators and a student change model, Cleveland's Yardstick Project

—these are among the efforts to gather the information and arrive at measures of effectiveness without which further systems analyses would be impossible. Moreover, program budgeting is beginning to enter the picture and has been introduced into school systems in New York, Memphis, Boston, Miami, Palo Alto, Phoenix, and other cities.

In this chapter the focus is less on administrative procedures, less on broad surveys, nationwide and statewide statistics, and cost-benefit studies, and more on "close-up" or "micro" studies of events taking place in the classrooms of individual schools. We will discuss some aspects of the evolution of the systems approach as developed by the Research and Technology Division of the System Development Corporation (SDC) in Santa Monica, California. The company, an offshoot of the RAND Corporation, was formed in 1957 mainly to apply advanced systems techniques to the nation's air defenses, and defense projects still make up the major part of its activities. In recent years, however, there has been a new emphasis on problems in the public area and notably on problems in education.

## SDC School Systems Studies

One project in particular, the first of its kind ever undertaken, has triggered a series of interesting and important studies. In the summer of 1963 a six-man research team headed by John Cogswell, a psychologist familiar with the workings of computers, started an investigation of the effects of educational innovation. A recent summary report indicates the original reason for conducting the study: "One major outcome of the new technology appeared to be that the educational system could better adapt itself to individual differences among students. . . . The traditional procedure of having 20 to 35 students spend the same amount of time together each day with one teacher, all progressing through the same set of materials at the same rate, seemed inconsistent with the developments taking place in instructional technology."

SDC scientists had already designed a special laboratory in which a computer could instruct up to twenty pupils at once in reading and other subjects, each pupil proceeding at his own pace. But they recognized the limitations of a laboratory setting and, even more important, the need for a basic study of the impact not merely of a single innovation, but of innovation in general, on school organization. Confronted with this problem, Cogswell and his associates decided to apply model techniques, developed to simulate a variety of air raids and fighter-bomber battles, to the less violent but more complicated activities of the classroom.

Arrangements were made to locate and communicate with schools which might be interested in the experiments. Model building and gathering data in education always depends on the participation of educators actively engaged in teaching, and in this case there was a special need for cooperation. Since no precedent existed for the sort of studies contemplated, everyone was in a sense starting from scratch. The following schools were selected for the project, after a survey based on a list of 200 schools known to be leaders in applying new methods: the Brigham Young University Laboratory School, Provo, Utah; the Buena Vista High School, Saginaw, Michigan; the Garber High School, Essexville, Michigan; the Nova

High School, Fort Lauderdale, Florida; and the Theodore High School, Theodore, Alabama.

## The Garber High School Model

The projects resulted in computer models of individual courses at each of these schools. For example Garber, a six-year junior–senior high school with about 700 students, is dedicated to the principle which says, "The individual learner should be permitted to move through as much subject matter as he can master"—and the mathematics department had organized its curriculum accordingly. Although students were required to spend a full school year on certain courses, other courses could be completed within a range of half a year to a year and a half. The new program started in 1965–66, the year of the SDC study, and the problem was to find out how it and similar programs would affect the operation of the school.

Jack Bratten, a member of the SDC team and an experienced simulation specialist, designed a model for running the next six years on a condensed time scale. Working closely with school administrators and mathematics teachers, he began to build his model from the ground up. The procedure consists of two essential stages which will be described in some detail since they are likely to be used increasingly in the years ahead, and since the basic conceptual work can be done without the benefit of mathematics or computers.

The first stage involved a period devoted to obtaining and organizing information. After studying the operation of the Garber mathematics department,

Bratten returned to Santa Monica and started his analysis by considering 100 first-year students enrolled in three courses for slow, medium and fast learners. At this point he had to consider the first of many possible distributions or "transition probabilities." For example, in the beginning, 20 students might be in the slow course, 55 in the medium course, and 25 in the fast course, and these proportions would change as students shifted from one course to another at various periods during semesters.

Things became more complicated during the second year, because more choices were open to students. All students had to spend their entire first year in one of the three levels of courses mentioned above. But two of the three second-year courses could be completed ahead of time, in half a year or three quarters of a year, and qualified students could then move ahead into certain advanced courses. Alternatives continued to multiply when it came to following the paths of students through a complete cycle of six years. The problem obviously involved a rather elaborate network of probable distributions.

Bratten developed the main features of the network in a series of pencilled branching-type flow diagrams with arrows showing shifts from one course to another. The diagrams served about the same purpose as the rough sketches an artist makes before undertaking a major work; they represented patterns of activity, the general structure of the problem. They also indicated information gaps, blanks in the network which had to be filled by another visit to the school and another round of data gathering. The first stage of the analysis ended with a finished diagram, a maze of paths and "decision points" showing the flow of students through twenty-nine different courses over a period of six years.

The next stage was to transform the static diagram into something dynamic, in effect to "animate" the flow chart on a computer. This was accomplished with the aid of a special simulation program developed by Donald Marsh and Frank Yett and known as EDSIM (EDucational SIMulation). EDSIM, like all computer programs is a generalized set of rules for expressing relationships common to an entire class of basic problems, a formalized procedure for building models involving student activities and changes in those activities through time. In a sense it does for the building of conceptual models what a set of assembly instructions does for the building of physical models.

EDSIM stipulates among other things that each student activity should be represented by a set of numbers—one number for the time of the activity, another for the percentage of students involved, and a third for the activity they will move on to next. For example 02–05–30–100–1 is a shorthand code for the following statement: of the students enrolled in course 102 for slow learners (Functional Mathematics I, coded as "02") five percent (05) shift on the thirtieth day of the course (30), and all of them (100, or 100 percent) shift to activity 1 (the code for course 100 for medium-speed learners). The statement 02–05–60–100–1 says that another five percent of the class make the same shift on the sixtieth day.

In all, there were more than 130 such coded statements. This information, which may be found in the finished flow diagram and in so-called distribution-rule tables, was transferred to special forms and key-punch operators in turn transferred the coded numbers to punchcards. A similar process is involved in preparing instructions, the orders which spell out exactly how the basic data are to be processed. In the case of the Garber study the orders specified that 100 simulated students should go through their first year and, as they passed into the second year, a new class of students should enter first-year courses —and so on until the original class had completed the entire six-year program, and the subsequent five classes had completed proportional parts of the curriculum. The instructions also allowed for an estimated enrollment increase of ten percent annually.

The resulting set of data and instruction punchcards represented the model of the mathematics curriculum. The cards were fed to a computer for a number of "debugging" trials conducted to detect and correct inaccuracies in transferring the information from tables to punchcards. (Unfortunately, human beings are very fallible and debugging generally takes considerably more computer time, at rentals of $300 to $500 an hour, than problem-solving.) Then the machine went through the simulation run for 1140 school days, or about 6.3 school years. The run took ten minutes of computing and produced a printout, a pile of paper three inches high and weighing about five pounds.

## Uses of the Garber Model

Analysis of the simulation record provided quantitative indications of what might be expected as far as enrollments, shifting and teaching and administrative problems are concerned. Enrollments were computed for each of the 29 mathematics courses, and a distribution printout revealed that practically all of the more advanced courses included students from three or four different grades. Furthermore, as might be expected, there was a great deal of shifting from one course to another; every fifteen days some 88 students entered or left a course. These figures provide some idea of what even a restricted form of individualized instruction means to teachers who have to deal with a situation in constant flux and with students of different age groups.

Clearly, the simulated students were much more on their own than real-life students in a traditional school environment. For example, they "decided" when they were ready to take tests, and the printout suggested that if all the mathematics courses were put on an individualized basis, an average of 55 tests would have to be administered every day. (Individualizing all courses offered by the school would require about 300 daily tests.) Although the computer did not "say" so directly, it certainly promoted its own usefulness by implication, since the only practical way of making all these tests results available is to let the computer do the bookkeeping.

As we have indicated in descriptions of other models, such figures are not to be taken too literally. More refined studies based on more recent school records would be required to provide truly precise data. But the simulation does suggest trends and orders of magnitude, and there are indications that it bears a significant relationship to reality. For example, it predicted a very low enrollment in one practical mathematics course, which is just what happened and the course has been dropped. Furthermore, it gave a general idea of the extra space required for individual

study, small-group discussions, student-teacher con-
sultations, and testing—and space limitations have indeed forced a change from flexible to conventional
scheduling.

But perhaps the most important effect of the study
has been something more intangible. It is a matter of
attitude rather than statistics. The very process of
discussing problems in systems terms and observing
Bratten in action has had an influence on planning.
Specifically it has influenced the preparation of new
curricula and new performance criteria in the departments of biology, humanities, and art. Quinton Cramer, Garber superintendent, has summarized the
results as follows: "The major benefit to us is that
we are thinking more about objectives that can be
measured. Also, we are beginning to look at problems
from a longer-range point of view."

## Individualized Instruction

Studies at the other schools followed the same general model-building pattern, but of course dealt with
a variety of different problems. At the Theodore High
School, another six-year school which stresses the importance of individualized instruction, the major effort
was concentrated on a single course rather than a
curriculum. Tenth-grade biology is a 35-week course
divided into ten work units, and pupils, using a study
guide, are free to select certain projects and to schedule themselves accordingly. But they are not free to
take as much time as they want, and a definite schedule is specified for the whole class. (The rule is that
work units 1 and 2 be finished by the end of the first
quarter, 3 through 5 by the end of the second quarter,

6 through 8 by the end of the third quarter, and 9 and 10 by the end of the year.)

The first phase of the Theodore study was to design a computer model which would simulate the performance of a hundred students under these conditions, and to check the model by comparing its computed results with actual class records. In general there was good agreement between the model and the real world. For example, the computer calculated that students would spend an average of 24.4 days on unit 1, 21 days on unit 3, 10.4 days on unit 7, and 9.9 days on unit 10—and actual performance records were 25.5, 21, 10.6 and 7.2 days respectively.

The next phase of the study involved a "what if" game, like the University of Toronto CAMPUS game described in the preceding chapter. The question: what would happen if the specified time constraints were removed, if students could work as fast or as slowly as they wanted, if the course were extended from 35 to 54 weeks (from one school year to about a year and a half)? A hundred simulated students were given individual learning rates based on records of the real-life course and, also in line with real-life behavior, the rates varied, being faster or slower than average about ten percent of the time.

The fastest learners soon found themselves way ahead of the rest of the class. One star student finished the course in fifteen weeks, four more students finished by the end of the twentieth week, and about a third of the entire class finished before the end of the school year. This simulated performance indicated one consequence of locking real-life students into a set schedule. It not only confirmed the suspicion that many students in the actual biology course were simply marking time and often did little or no work, but also indicated the probable extent of the practice.

The simulation also provided an interesting evaluation of the go-as-you-please course. The price of teaching students beyond the conventional school year was 332 extra student-weeks of instruction. But 425 student-weeks were saved by permitting faster learners to finish ahead of time, so the longer simulated course justified itself on a "cost-benefit" basis. Furthermore, 82 percent of the students completed the longer course as compared with only 54 percent for the actual course. SDC investigators concluded: "If progress in the actual biology course were to be based on course content and student ability, the 35-week normal school year is not an optimal period."

At Theodore as at Garber simulation research has drawn attention to the systems approach. A social studies course has been organized along the general lines of the biology course and, partly as a result of the SDC research, it was decided to establish a minimum-work rule to reduce the tendency of faster learners to mark time. But the most unusual by-product of the research is that John Jackson, the principal of the school, and several of his associates have developed preliminary plans for a computer model that would follow the progress of more than 1500 students through all classes and grades.

## Other School Simulations

Further simulations were run at the other schools. At Brigham Young, for example, a model of the ninth-grade algebra class calculated the rates of progress for fast, medium, and slow learners—and indicated that the slow students would take more and more of the teacher's time as the course progressed, a result that checked with actual experience and placed renewed emphasis on the need for special planning in such cases. At Buena Vista, which features team teaching and an elaborate closed-circuit television system, studies of an eleventh-grade English course produced a model which is available to analyze the effects on student performance of increasing or reducing the number of weekly "tele-lessons" and varying other conditions.

We have indicated some of the effects of the simulation project on policies and attitudes at the five schools, and there would have undoubtedly been more extensive results if time and funds had permitted continuing systems analyses. Indeed, the project points up the need to establish permanent systems offices, similar to those in Toronto and Berkeley, in large school districts as well as at the state level. As far as SDC is concerned, there have been benefits in the form of new insights into problems of organizing for individualized instruction, and a fuller understanding of the use and potentialities of model building and other systems methods.

There have also been more direct results. The five-school studies brought a new and heightened awareness of a point basic to the creation of an atmosphere in which every student has a chance to develop and express his unique abilities at his own pace. In such an environment it is no longer possible to rely solely on mid-year and final examinations and interim quizzes, administered periodically and *en masse* to entire classes. The complete inappropriateness of such procedures is implied in the Garber simulation indicating that at least 55 tests would have to be administered every day in an individualized mathematics curriculum, and the Brigham Young and Theodore studies point in the same direction.

Truly individualized instruction implies the existence of a system sensitive to the current and changing needs of individual students. According to John Coulson, associate director of SDC's Education and Training Staff: "If we are really serious about providing such instruction, we have no choice but to track students as they move through their work. In a good tracking or monitoring system you are constantly assessing the individual's needs—and right now monitoring may be even more critical than developing educational materials. After all, we cannot know what to prescribe until we have a far better idea of the nature of those needs."

These considerations have led to a new research effort. Coulson and Bratten are developing a tracking system which is ultimately intended for widespread use and therefore involves a minimum of change in teaching routines. In fact, the system has already passed beyond the blueprint stage. Trials have been under way this year at two local schools, Brentwood and Roosevelt, under a contract with the Southwest Regional Laboratory for Educational Research and Development in Los Angeles (one of a network of twenty such organizations established throughout the country by the Office of Education).

A total of 130 first-grade pupils are being monitored in reading and arithmetic. Three times a week groups of about a dozen pupils sit at their desks, tests before them, during periods when their teachers are working with other groups. They are equipped with earphones and follow recorded voice instructions item by item. For example a reading test designed to measure visual discrimination includes a line with the words "mother," "airplane," and "apple," and under each word there is a blank oval space. The pupil must match one of these words with the word "airplane" appearing to the left of the line and must indicate his choice by filling in the appropriate oval space with a black pencil. A single test may consist of thirty such items on half a dozen pages the size of a sheet of regular typewriter paper.

The tests are collected, brought to SDC headquarters, and fed into a moving-belt optical scanner which has photoelectric cells to sense the black pencil marks and can process 2000 pages an hour. The scanner automatically translates item-by-item results into coded signals that are transmitted directly into a computer. The computer then goes through a high-speed analysis of the information, printing dated progress reports which teachers use to keep track of performance records and to help them in selecting further tests to meet the particular needs of individual pupils.

The printouts provide a variety of important facts. General data are supplied about group achievement, together with the score of the pupil who did best in the test and the score of the poorest pupil. But the group analysis goes deeper. Each reading test is designed to measure a number of different abilities—visual discrimination, word recognition (matching words and pictures), auditory discrimination, word comprehension, sentence meaning, and so on. There are also items with built-in "distractors," items showing whether the pupil actually recognizes the word as a distinct entity or is going by false clues. For example,

he may match "apple" and "airplane" because they
both start with "a," or "apple" and "chair" because
they both have five letters. The printout indicates
high and low achievement in each of the abilities
being tested and recommends extra "group word
practice," "pronunciation—initial B," and other remedial activities.

Incidentally, a great deal of preparatory work went
into designing the printouts. They must not only con-
tain the information which teachers want, but the
information must be presented clearly and concisely
in a familiar format. So one step was to test various
types of format by simulating a class being tracked,
and creating simulated printouts. This meant building
a model with techniques developed during the five-
school project—a model of eleven pupils taking up to
40 tests each, with about 30 items in each test.
Brentwood and Roosevelt teachers criticized early
simulated printouts and helped design improved versions. In fact, to participate in this work two of the
teachers became temporary members of the SDC
team last summer.

## Student-Computer Interaction

The tracking system also includes an "interactive"
feature, a way of permitting two-way communication
between computer and teacher. In other words, the
teacher can draw on the vast store of information
which exists in the machine's memory files but which
cannot be included in the standard printout. (A printout containing all the stored information would be
larger than several New York telephone directories.)
She can go to a teletype machine connected by tele-

phone lines to an SDC computer, type out her school and class, and engage in the following sort of dialogue:

COMPUTER: PLEASE TYPE YOUR NAME
TEACHER: JANET ARMSTRONG
COMPUTER: WHAT KIND OF INFORMATION DO YOU WANT?
TEACHER: ? (Meaning "I don't know the choices")
COMPUTER: CHOOSE ONE OF THE FOLLOWING:
    A. SUMMARY OF CLASS
    B. INDIVIDUAL STUDENT HISTORY
TEACHER: B
COMPUTER: TYPE STUDENTS NAME OR NUMBER
TEACHER: 235
COMPUTER: WHAT KIND OF DISPLAY DO YOU WANT FOR LINDA WEST?
TEACHER: ?
COMPUTER: CHOOSE ONE OF THE FOLLOWING:
    1. SCORES ON GENERAL OBJECTIVES
    2. SCORES ON SPECIFIC OBJECTIVES
TEACHER: 2
COMPUTER: SPECIFY TESTS FOR WHICH SCORES ARE DESIRED
TEACHER: ALL

The computer then prints out the information requested. Incidentally, if the teacher had been thoroughly familiar with the procedure she could simply have replied to the first question with : B 235 2 ALL.

Two important technical developments make such dialogues possible. The first is the design of a special natural computer language known as PLANIT (Programming Language for Interactive Teaching), which teachers can use to communicate with machines on an easy "man to man" basis, expressing themselves in regular English. A generation or so ago, in the Neanderthal days of man-machine communications, all messages were written out in numbers instead of words. That meant learning a specialized and distinctly unnatural language so that once you decided what you wanted to say, you could translate it into numerical codes which a computer could "understand." Nowadays the computer itself can be programmed to do the translating,·which is about what was done in formulating PLANIT.

The second major development is known as timesharing. When a teacher uses the teletype terminal at Brentwood or Roosevelt, she feels that she has its complete and undivided "attention" throughout the dialogue. After all, the exchange of questions and answers generally proceeds without undue delay, exactly as if she were engaging in a face-to-face conversation with a consultant. But a truly full-time consultation would never be practical. It would represent an enormous inefficiency and extravagance, because of the discrepancy between computer speeds and the speed of human thinking.

Suppose it takes only five seconds to type, "Linda isn't doing well in her pronunciation exercises," which is reasonably fast—for a human being. But from the machine's point of view five seconds is a long long time; in that period it could be performing millions of arithmetic or logical operations. If the teacher stopped to think for a whole minute or so, and the machine had to wait and do nothing while she thought, the inefficiency would be appalling. In a minute it could do more work than a man at a desk-type calculator could do in more than eight months.

Time-sharing is a solution to this problem, pioneered by scientists at SDC and the Massachusetts Institute of Technology. In effect the computer behaves something like a chess master playing a number of games simultaneously against a group of amateurs. He stops at one board, looks over the situation, makes a move and then passes to the next board, repeating the circuit until the games are finished. Similarly, the computer automatically shifts from one use to another, devoting a fraction of a second to each user and then passing to the next. While it serves the teacher it may also be serving other specialists concerned with air defenses, artificial-satellite orbits, city planning, fingerprint identification of criminals, and so on. If the time per user is half a second and there are twenty users, it comes around every ten seconds which, considering the time required for thinking and typing, is frequently enough to give the illusion of continuous full-time interaction.

## Computer-Aided Instruction

The new tracking system is actually a form of computer-assisted instruction. Studies in this rapidly expanding field are also proceeding at Stanford University, the University of Illinois, the University of Pittsburgh, the International Business Machines Corporation, and other organizations. One of the most advanced projects has been developed at Stanford and involves a special computer and individual terminals installed in the school. The computer instructs many pupils at once, presenting printed and pictorial material on screens at each terminal, tailoring specific instructional material to the strengths and weaknesses of the individual pupil—and compiling complete records of individual performance.

Some day such highly automated systems will be installed in schools throughout the nation and will be used as routinely as blackboards and slide projectors are today. However, there is a more immediate need for less complex systems that can be maintained by regular school personnel without massive financial and technical assistance from outside agencies, and without drastic changes in classroom or administrative procedures. The SDC system is designed for this purpose. Furthermore, the hope is that a monitoring system put into use in the near future will stimulate a widespread demand for good remedial material and thus will be a first step toward the more individualized instruction made possible by computer-aided techniques.

The five-school project has also led to a further study, and a particularly important one. There is another kind of monitoring which may be at least as important as that under development at the Brentwood and Roosevelt schools—the kind that involves the future of the pupil, his long-range goals, and the significance of his current progress in terms of those goals. Over and over again discussions with teachers and administrators emphasized the need for more and better counseling, and drew attention to the potential role of the computer in this process.

The interesting thing is that the use of computers, frequently cited as a sign of the trend toward regimentation and conformity in our times, actually represents one of the most promising ways of "humanizing" the counseling process. The computer offers a way of providing more individualized counseling, as well as more individualized instruction, to more pupils—and this possibility is being explored under the direction of John Cogswell. He points out that as far as the present situation is concerned the counselor often tends to behave more like a computer than a sensitive advisor, and a badly used computer at that. The whole problem is exemplified in the remark of an overworked and frustrated counselor who reported: "I don't have time to listen to a kid; I just give him information."

For more than two years Cogswell and his associates have been working with two San Fernando Valley schools in the Los Angeles school system, the James Monroe High School (3600 students, six full-time and four part-time counselors), and the Sepulveda Junior High School (1800 students, four full-time counselors and one part-time). They built a model containing information about the skills, backgrounds, test scores, and goals of a hundred simulated students and, by a series of man-machine dialogues similar to those currently being used in the Brentwood-Roosevelt monitoring system, demonstrated to the counselors the possibilities and limitations of computers.

They have also tried a unique and successful experiment in practical communications. A clinical psychologist was invited to sit in on discussions with the ten James Monroe counselors, as a kind of observer and guide. He made only a few comments, but his presence encouraged free and animated exchanges in a series of meetings ending with a "marathon" meeting that lasted for twelve successive hours. "The observer made it easier for us," Cogswell recalls. "We didn't feel responsible for running things; he was doing that. As a result we reached a stage in understanding and the sharing of ideas which we might never have reached even if we had met many more times."

## Computerized Counseling

A computer system incorporating some of the ideas has just gone into operation at the schools. The machine does much of the record keeping and routine work which currently bogs the counselor down. It includes all student information, data about marks, health, extracurricular activities, and previous counseling sessions, and checks the information periodically to keep it up to date. Also if a student has neglected to fill out an application form or sign up for a particular course or come for an interview, the machine automatically prints out appropriate reminder cards for him and his counselor. He may obtain information about vocations or colleges from the computer by engaging in dialogues on a time-sharing basis at a "counseling terminal." These and other features make it possible for counselors to devote more of their time to direct talks with students, perhaps fifty percent more time.

In general, developments like those going on in the Los Angeles area illustrate the problems that must be solved in building technology into schools. The new art of simulation, of putting plans and hypotheses to the test in computers on a condensed time scale, is one of a number of innovations that are changing education before our eyes. Technology makes many things possible, but the most encouraging sign is an awareness of purposes. One thing seems to have been learned from the example of industry, and from early misplaced efforts to emulate industry—the danger of dehumanizing human beings in the process of bringing in machines. There will be no "dark Satanic mills" in education as long as the central objective is to provide students with the special materials and attention they require as individuals.

Teachers, counselors, and administrators have the ultimate responsibility for preserving and promoting this objective within individual schools. To guide the systems specialist in his research, to make their full contribution to the future, they must be more than nominal "members of the team," consultants who are consulted for form's sake only and after the fact. They must play an active part in designing innovations of all sorts, in creating and testing innovations instead of merely accepting available teaching materials or choosing among available materials. This is perhaps the major lesson to be learned from productive collaborations such as those evolving at SDC and other systems-oriented organizations.

# CHAPTER 8

# THE NEXT DECADE

THE USE of the systems approach in education is a very recent development. Certain pioneer experiments were conducted a decade or more ago, but the major studies, practically all the work discussed in the preceding chapters, is a matter mainly of the past few years. The really big push came with the White House Executive Order of 1965 which stipulated that all federal programs should be evaluated by modern planning-budgeting techniques—and, incidentally, created an estimated 6000 new jobs for systems specialists in Washington alone (about 3000 of which are still unfilled).

The order also created a new atmosphere for planning in education and other public areas, a sense of urgency about problems which had previously been tackled on a large scale during depression times only. Under such conditions rapid changes may be expected. Most of today's important systems techniques are in the process of transition. They are evolving just as the mathematical techniques typical of early World War II days evolved in response to the wider problems of military and industrial strategies. Even more significant, today's complexities demand the invention of entirely new techniques, some of which are already beginning to take shape.

At the technological level the systems approach is certain to benefit increasingly from progress in the computer sciences. We are in the midst of changes so radical that their long-range effects can be predicted only in the most general terms. According to Anthony Oettinger of the Harvard Program on Technology and Society, we are amplifying our intelligence enormously: "Computers are capable of profoundly affecting science by stretching human reason and intuition, much as telescopes or microscopes extend human vision. I suspect that the ultimate effects of this stretching will be as far-reaching as the effects of the invention of writing."

One of the most important developments in electronics is known as "miniaturization," the art of cramming more and more circuitry into less and less space. The first of the modern high-speed electronic computers, the Eniac of 1946, was an engineering dinosaur. It weighed more than thirty tons, occupied the area of a tennis court, and required an air-conditioning system to dissipate the heat generated by its 20,000 vacuum tubes. Today a far more powerful model may be smaller than a single file cabinet—and the future is indicated in a new experimental device, a crystal wafer about the size of a half-dollar piece which includes some 200 built-in circuits each made up of a dozen resistors and other components.

Probably within a decade such devices will make possible the manufacture of extremely compact computers which will outperform present-day versions by a considerable margin and will sell or rent for a fraction of the cost. One result, of course, will be the widespread use of computer-assisted instruction and computerized library information services. But the new machines can be expected to serve planners as well as teachers and students. They are certain to provide the additional memory capacity and speed required for the running of more complicated and more realistic simulations. Also, advanced programming techniques are being developed to help save time in designing such models, a development which should compensate in part at least for the shortage of systems specialists.

## The Educator-Computer Dialogue

As far as the near future is concerned, say the next two or three years, we can expect a sharp rise in dialogues between educators and computers, question-and-answer sessions like those described in the preceding chapter. Although enough experience has already been accumulated to indicate the value of computer models in exploring alternatives on a "what if" basis, the procedure has been seriously limited in one respect. As a general rule, several hours or even two or three days may pass between the preparation of a problem and the solution in the form of a complete printout.

For instance, consider a case discussed earlier—the use of the Toronto CAMPUS model to explore the effect, on next year's space and faculty requirements, of increasing teaching loads by two hours a week. That problem required rather less than a minute of actual computing time. But investigators had to wait overnight to obtain the solution, because there were other demands on the machine, and the university computer center processed problems by batches according to definite schedules. As a consequence of such delays the process amounts to asking a question and then waiting hours for an answer, which hardly makes for a spontaneous flow of ideas.

Time-sharing is one way of overcoming this difficulty. An investigator working "on line" with a computer simulation model can start to teletype a question, change his mind and cancel it, and then substitute another question. After the machine responds promptly with its teletyped answer, he is free to try a variation of the same question, or an entirely different idea which may have occurred to him on the spur of the moment. Engaging in such an exchange is a strange and vaguely disturbing experience. You feel as if you were in a science-fiction world talking with a robot, which in a sense is precisely what you are doing. Programs are being prepared for even more realistic conversations, enabling a computer to converse far more "creatively" than it does at present. Upon analyzing a question it may come up with the following sort of reply: "That problem will take three minutes and forty seconds of computing time, and it may not yield the information you want. Have you considered trying Procedure X?"

Systems specialists have not yet made large-scale use of time-sharing in studying educational problems, but some notable results have been obtained in other areas. For example, not long ago executives at a large electronics company had an exhaustive dialogue with a computer programmed to simulate company operations, asking several hundred questions in an effort to reduce costs for a new radar unit. They started with the notion of reducing investments in engineering and development, but decided to try changes in sales policies and other factors when the original plan seemed to have less effect than expected. Finally they discovered that in this particular case the greatest saving, amounting to about twenty-five percent, could be obtained by reducing manufacturing time from fourteen to twelve months—a course that would probably not have been explored in precomputer days.

Another so-called planning model, this one involving auto sales and dealer locations, has been developed by John Little and his associates at the Massachusetts Institute of Technology. Next to his office desk is a teletype console connected to a remote time-shared computer, and on the wall a chart of the Chicago region divided into 140 marketing areas or "cells." Each cell contains a number of differently colored dots indicating the sites of agencies selling the eight major makes of car: Buick, Chevrolet, Dodge, Ford, Oldsmobile, Plymouth, Pontiac, Rambler.

Little signed in on the console, typing out a coded statement identifying himself and his model, and began talking to the machine:

| | |
|---|---|
| COMPUTER: | BEGIN PLEASE |
| LITTLE: | MOVE DLR 222 to CELL 131 |
| COMPUTER: | DODG DLR NUMBER 222 HAS BEEN MOVED TO CELL 131   CONTINUE |
| LITTLE: | CHANGE FOR DLR 222 (shorthand for "How will this move affect sales?") |

| COMPUTER: | DODG DLR 222 | SALES | PENE-TRATION |
|---|---|---|---|
| | FORMER SYSTEM | 82 | .17126 |
| | PRESENT SYSTEM | 73 | .15391 |
| | NET LOSS | 9 | .01735 |
| | CONTINUE | | |

The conversation included a number of other what-if games, the effect of the move on the sales of local Ford dealers, on the sales of all makes of cars throughout the Chicago region, and so on. Models based on the same general principles could be used to investigate a variety of location problems such as those concerning the sites for new schools or "educational parks."

In a recent experiment about thirty college administrators participated in a conference on planning models for universities. They sat at the usual consoles and played the game of trying to operate a hypothetical five-school university as efficiently as possible over a five-year period—varying the size and composition of faculty, faculty-student ratios, tuition, and other factors, and evaluating alternatives. In many respects this session represented the sort of process characteristic of the Toronto and Berkeley models, plus the time-sharing dialogue feature. It served as another demonstration of the fact that planning models are one of the major contributions of computer science to the systems approach.

## The Crucial Problem of Implementation

New techniques will also have to be developed in the political sphere. In the last analysis all the scientific ingenuity in the world, all the contributions of modern technology, are nullified in a systems study if that study fails in its essential objective—to help achieve positive results in the real world. It is a sad and potent fact of life that in the public area such failures are extremely common and may indeed represent the rule rather than the exception. At least half of all federal programs designed for the public welfare are never carried out, which is not an outstanding batting average. The reasons for this unimpressive record are chiefly political. The programs offer benefits to some people but also step on the toes of others, or threaten to, and are accordingly cut down to size.

At one time, when ivory towers were more popular among scientists than they are nowadays, the systems scientist tended to assume a what-can-you-expect attitude toward this unimpressive record. He believed not only that he could do nothing about it but also that it was not his place to try. "After all, I'm just a technician" expressed the prevailing feeling of resignation. Things are changing, however. The urgency of the times somehow makes it less easy to sit back and watch carefully conceived programs go down the drain and pass it all off philosophically.

This does not imply that the systems profession is about to organize itself into a lobbying agency. It is hardly a matter of the profession deciding to enter the political arena. The real questions are basically technical ones. Can analytical techniques be applied specifically to the intensely political problems of getting things done? Can the opposition to programs stemming from the systems approach be overcome or effectively reduced by the use of the systems approach itself? The success of much future planning may depend on the answers to such questions. It is not enough to build more realistic computer models. Systems specialists will also have to deal more realistically with people and public opinion, which means inevitably coming to grips with the forces of human conflict.

A pioneer study in this largely unexplored area

has been prepared by two investigators at Case Western Reserve University, fittingly enough by a systems specialist and a political economist—Burton Dean, who has been mentioned earlier in a number of connections, and Samuel Mantel, professor of economics. They became interested in the fate of a proposal to run a freeway through one of the suburbs of a large city (unidentified, for political reasons). From the engineering and city-planning standpoints the route was the best available, but the proposal faced strong local opposition.

## Exploring Opposition-Reducing Techniques

The study, a combined case history and model for future application, is based on the following principle: "The cost of reducing opposition is a proper part of the total cost of implementing a public project." To arrive at this cost Dean and Mantel consulted transportation planners, and obtained from them a list of fourteen community organizations which had opposed the proposal. They also evaluated the relative power of the groups. Three of them, including organizations that ranked high in the city government hierarchy, received a "fatal" rating because any one of them alone could have defeated the proposal.

Of the eleven "nonfatal" groups (citizens' committees organized especially to resist the proposed project: school boards, conservationists, the press, local Audubon Society chapters, and so on) two were rated "very powerful," eight "medium powerful" and one "weak." Then the investigators went through a more intensive quantitative evaluation process, ending up with a list of all the groups in the order of their relative effectiveness as opposers, as well as estimates of the relative power of various coalitions among the nonfatal groups. Furthermore, the reasons for opposition were identified by consulting the planners and by making a survey of home owners in the community.

As an example, suppose that a preliminary survey reveals that Group A opposes a freeway because it would cut through a popular park area, increase the traffic load on city streets, make it more difficult for children to reach local schools, separate friends, and require the relocation of homes. Given such data, planners can estimate the costs of measures designed to overcome Group A's objections—subsidies for building new parks, overpasses, and wider streets; additional indemnities to families having to move; funds for developing and disseminating propaganda to help reduce fears about loss of access to friends; and so on.

The next step would be to evaluate the effectiveness of a number of alternative "package" budgets for putting all the measures into effect, in terms of the probabilities of success associated with each budget. For instance, in the case of Group A a total budget of $2.25 million might have only one chance in ten of overcoming opposition, while for larger budgets of $7.5 and $34 million chances might be fifty-fifty and nine in ten respectively. Similar estimates would be made for all opposing groups, and analyses indicating the "anti-opposition" or "opposition reduction" costs of each of a number of possible freeway routes would help planners decide on an optimum route to be recommended and adopted. This is the sort of information upon which detailed research can be based. According to the Dean-Mantel study it should be obtained during the planning of any public project likely to arouse serious opposition, and that includes practically all major urban redevelopment projects.

Dean and Mantel first reported this work more than a year ago at a meeting held in Washington, D.C., a most appropriate location considering the political overtones of their research. Their audience consisted largely of systems specialists and urban planners who are deeply concerned with federal programs and well aware of the problems of winning support for those programs. The odds are that anti-opposition techniques will become increasingly important not only at the local level but also within various federal agencies. Indeed, there has been some talk of similar research on the make-up and relative power of opposition groups within Congress.

## Systems Analyst and Decision Maker

Generally speaking, the nature of the relationship between the systems specialist and those responsible for major decisions is critical. If the relationship is not close, his work tends to be academic and remote and, as far as getting things done is concerned, amounts to little more than treading water. An official close to the workings of a large state department of education recently attributed its slow progress in developing new plans to just such a situation: "The department has some first-rate people who appreciate what's needed and what can be done. But they have no resources, no leverage. They're not hooked into the power structure."

On the other hand, the advantages of a close and continuing relationship have been demonstrated in a number of instances. The fact that Toronto's Office of Institutional Research reports directly to, and has the full support of, administrators at the highest university level has already been cited, and represents an important factor in the record achieved by this group. On a national scale, Sweden provides a case in point. Its educational system, which has served as a model for planners in the United States and abroad, incorporates effective procedures for converting proposed reforms into legislation—including government-sponsored conferences attended by educators, political and labor leaders, and representatives of other public groups.

But neither political leverage nor technological advances are sufficient by themselves. The future of the systems approach depends on new knowledge as well as new legislative procedures and new devices. A need exists for more research on group behavior, on the basic mechanisms that affect our decisions and our reactions to one another and to new ideas. For example, there is Cogswell's pioneer experiment at SDC, involving the presence of a clinical psychologist to encourage free and frank discussions between counselors and investigators. There is also the problem of obtaining expert judgment, an indispensible element throughout the systems process from the defining of objectives to the choice of a course of action. Since no individual is all-knowing, that generally involves attempts to arrive at a consensus by assembling a number of experts, and difficulties may arise at precisely this stage.

Conferences enjoy a rather low reputation when it comes to achieving a meeting of minds and getting something done. Some years ago a widely read scientific journal published a humorous article on the mathematics of committees, boards, and panels. The most memorable feature of the article was a curve which, purporting to show the relationship between efficiency and committee size, reached a peak at slightly less than one member and was interpreted by the author as a strong argument for limiting committees to a single person at most.

Allowing for understandable exaggeration, there may be some basis for this conclusion and for the general notion that meetings are often a waste of time, at least meetings of persons specializing in the same field. Apparently experts do not always behave rationally among their peers. Like all of us, they play roles to the detriment of their own wisdom. They may strut a bit, and give voice to judgments based more on the urge to impress than on careful consideration, and oppose novel ideas chiefly to preserve their prestige. They may either cling aggressively to their own ideas or yield to majority opinion, not necessarily because they are really convinced but because they want to be regarded as good guys.

There is nothing at all new about such behavior. Aristophanes made fun of it more than two thousand years ago, and it was probably well known to the earliest members of the species. The crucial point is that times have changed. We cannot be content simply to regard the behavior of experts, fondly or otherwise, as foibles of "human nature" (whatever that is). We have reached a stage in our history, in our evolution, where we must make the most of our intellectual resources. Wisdom is more than ever a collective thing, more the possession of groups and less of individuals however talented—and it has become so important that we can no longer afford the luxury of not taking it as pure and undiluted as possible.

## Consensus and the Delphi Method

Research on the consensus problem was conducted in the early 1950's at the RAND Corporation. Olaf Helmer and his colleagues developed a special way of obtaining group opinions about certain urgent defense problems, and christened it the "Delphi" method in honor of the oracle of Apollo. An unclassified version of this method was published about five years ago, and has stimulated a good deal of research since then. It is intended to avoid personality pressures and related complications and to get at expert opinion without bringing the experts together face-to-face. They are consulted individually, as a rule by questionnaire.

There are a number of variations on the Delphi theme, but the general idea is to prepare successive rounds of questions designed to elicit progressively more carefully considered group opinions. The procedure, which involves some rather sophisticated ways of arranging and presenting information, may take a form such as the following:

1) The first questionnaire may call for a list of opinions involving experienced judgment, say a list of predictions or recommended activities.

2) On the second round each expert receives a copy of the list, and is asked to rate or evaluate each item by some such criterion as importance, probability of success, and so on.

3) The third questionnaire includes the list and the ratings, indicates the consensus if any, and in effect asks the experts either to revise their opinions or else to specify their reasons for remaining outside the consensus.

4) The fourth questionnaire includes list, ratings, the consensus, and minority opinions. It provides a final chance for the revision of opinions.

The procedure generally succeeds in its objective of encouraging convergence of opinion, or at least a majority opinion and a clearly defended minority opinion. Helmer has used it to conduct an extensive world-of-tomorrow survey of predicted long-range developments in science, automation, space research, and other areas. For example, one panel of experts was asked on its first questionnaire to list "major inventions and scientific breakthroughs in areas of special concern to you which you regard as both urgently needed and feasible within the next fifty years." The forecasts included mining the ocean floor, breeding apes and other intelligent animals for low-grade labor, the widespread use of personality-changing drugs, the invention of antigravity devices, and forty-odd other items.

The second round requested estimates of the probability of each item occurring within each of a number of time intervals, the most remote being "1997–2000," "later than 2013" and "never." Subsequent questionnaires narrowed the range of opinions in most cases. For example, consider estimates concerning the widespread use of personality-changing drugs. The third questionnaire noted that no satisfactory consensus had been reached and, among other things, asked the experts to predict by what year there would be a fifty percent chance of the practice occurring. They were also asked to explain their reasoning if they selected a "fifty percent" year before 1987 or after 2013 (or never). The fourth questionnaire included the majority opinion that the fifty-percent year would be

2000, the minority opinion that social resistance and the need for more research would delay the practice by at least a half a century, and provided one more opportunity to revise forecasts. It yielded a fairly good consensus, half of the experts predicting widespread use of the drugs before 1983 and three quarters before the year 2000.

Of course, this long-range survey cannot immediately answer the basic question about the quality or validity of the method—does it yield wiser or more accurate group opinions than conventional meetings? We will not know for at least two or three more generations whether the experts' predictions about scientific breakthroughs jibe with actual developments. But studies of short-term predictions have been conducted at the University of California in Los Angeles where twenty graduate business students participated in a Delphi study during the fall of 1965. They forecast the gross national product, defense expenditures, and fourteen other business indexes; and the forecasts were later checked with what actually happened.

The students generally arrived at good group judgments after four rounds of questionnaires. Although they were far off on certain indexes (for example, predicting a drop of a billion dollars in the federal budget as compared with an actual rise of $200 million), in most cases they achieved an accuracy of ten percent or better. But the significant finding, and the point of the study, was their performance as compared not to reality—but to twenty students who filled out non-Delphi questionnaires which asked for forecasts only and did not request explanations or provide feedback information about

majority and minority opinions. In thirteen out of
sixteen cases the Delphi group did better than the
non-Delphi group; the non-Delphi group did better
in two cases; and in one case both groups made the
same prediction.

## The Delphi Method and Education

These and other studies indicate the effectiveness
of the Delphi method. Its power seems to lie in the
fact that it creates some of the most important
elements of an ideal debate. It provides an impersonal anonymous setting in which opinions can be
expressed in clear terms and heeded before the voic-
ing of criticisms and counteropinions, a setting in
which ideas can be modified on the basis of reason
rather than prestige or a desire to climb on the band-
wagon. As far as the systems approach is concerned,
Delphi-type techniques will be used more and more
because of the increase in public projects which depend especially on consensus and compromise and
the judgments of experienced administrators.

The results of a 1965 pilot experiment suggest the
potential value of such techniques in education. Three
groups of educators who had recently participated in
various discussions of innovations filled out Delphi
questionnaires and produced a list of ninety-three proposed reforms, together with estimates of what the
federal government would have to spend during a
five-year period to carry out each reform indepen-
dently. The participants also prepared a five-year
budget totalling $10 billion, allocating the funds among
the various proposals. The following are some features
of the final consensus as summarized by Helmer:

1) The largest single item was $3 billion to raise teachers' salaries.

2) The two next largest items totalled $1.65 billion and were aimed at increasing student participation—encouraging life-long education by awarding grants to promising adults for educational leaves, and providing public-school education for children under five years old.

3) In general, experiments with teaching machines, developing measures of teaching ability and the effectiveness of innovations, and other exploratory studies, received large-scale support.

4) Costly new equipment, including audiovisual material available for individual use and computerized libraries, was allotted some $700 million—"not nearly as large a share as it might have absorbed, possibly reflecting the opinion that more experimental work should precede large-scale adoption of new devices."

5) The category "reorganization of instruction and programs" included twenty-two separate proposals, and practically all of them received budgetary support.

6) All three groups rejected five high-cost proposals: subsidizing private schools, subsidizing on-the-job industrial training, reversing the trend toward larger schools, providing full-pay sabbaticals to teachers, and increasing the salaries of high-school teachers to college levels.

It is not difficult to see how such studies can be used at every stage of the systems approach, and particularly in the design of planning models to test various proposals and combinations of proposals. But other new techniques will have to be developed as the approach is called on to deal with problems of broader and broader scope. For example, there is a new program known as the Information System for Vocational Decisions, which is directed jointly by the

Harvard Graduate School of Education, the Newton Public School System, and New England Education Data. It represents a radical expansion of the entire concept of counseling, moving about as far as possible from the notion of the counselor as someone concerned chiefly with jobs or colleges for high-school seniors.

The aim is to establish a complete "mediating environment," a progressive and expanding relationship that would start in the earliest school years and continue through college and beyond. The individual student will learn to use dialogues with a time-shared computer system as an aid in thinking about the future, understanding himself, exploring career possibilities, and making decisions. This program, currently being developed with the assistance of teachers and counselors, conceives of vocational planning as a lifetime process and as such will involve systems techniques whose scope is nothing less than a lifetime. Indeed all programs that formally recognize the continuing quality of education demand increasingly the evaluation of such things as fulfillment and self-respect as well as more conventional measures of effectiveness.

## The Student and Life-Planning

As a final point in this introductory survey, it is important to reemphasize and further elaborate on matters discussed in the preceding chapter. The focus of all the technology and advanced thinking must be on the student and what he is learning. Applying the results of research on miniaturization and time-sharing, building political strategies into systems studies, making the most of consultants and group wisdom, expanding the notion of counseling toward genuine life-planning for the individual—these and associated developments serve the fundamental purpose of communication, bringing information and insights of the right sort to the right students at the right times.

The future will certainly bring about further changes in the nature and content of specific courses. The preceding chapter is devoted entirely to problems that can be expected to arise as a consequence of extensive planning. It indicates how computer models, based on detailed studies and simulations of classroom situations, may be used in studying the impact of educational innovations intended to give fuller expression to individual differences among students. It deals with a variety of experiments on new teaching methods, the design of new courses, and methods of evaluating the effectiveness of the courses.

These experiments call for the direct participation of teachers and educators. For example, consider the tracking system currently being developed for first-grade students in the Los Angeles area. The system involves a number of weekly tests in reading and arithmetic. Teachers working with System Development Corporation investigators played a central role in designing the tests and determining the content of courses. A major aim of the project is to arouse interest in new courses, to stimulate a wider demand for fresh approaches and fresh material, not only in the Los Angeles school system but throughout the country. (This is one reason why the Office of Education is interested in the project.)

The encouraging thing is that considerable work is already being done in an effort to improve individual courses—work which exemplifies the spirit and basic purposes, if not always the formal techniques, of the systems approach. For example, many important developments owe a great deal to a broad and exceedingly ambitious plan which dates back more than a decade. In 1956 a group of physicists and educators, working under the direction of Jerrold Zacharias of the Massachusetts Institute of Technology, held their first large-scale meeting to discuss ways of improving the teaching of science in high school. The chief reason for the meeting was a general agreement that existing courses were based on outmoded viewpoints and that attempts to make up for the deficiencies were largely of a patchwork nature.

The group, known as the Physical Science Study Committee (PSSC), concentrated on a one-year physics course for high school juniors or seniors. It decided that the course would consist of four sections dealing first with basic concepts (time, measurement, atomic structure, and so on), then with waves and optics, the laws of motion and the kinetic theory of heat, and electromagnetic phenomena. Scientists and teachers at different institutions undertook the organization and development of the sections, which were to meet the following criteria, as stated in a formal statement of the project:

1) To stress major achievements of physics, such as the great conservation principles.

2) To give insight into the way in which these powerful ideas were conceived, nurtured and sometimes overthrown by even more powerful ideas.

3) To present a unified story in which the interconnections within physics were brought to light.

4) To show physics as a human activity comparable in significance with the humanities, the languages and the other major studies of high school students.

Thus, from the very beginning the PSSC effort involved clear statements of objectives and criteria. Furthermore, an exhaustive inventory was made of alternative methods and materials that would promote the attainment of those objectives. The program included not only the preparation of a new textbook— but also the development of film strips and motion pictures, special laboratory apparatus as well as simple equipment that can be made from materials obtained at neighborhood stores and at home, teachers' manuals, a series of paperback books for collateral reading, and so on. Provisions were also made for evaluating the program. For example, in 1958–59 more than 12,500 students took the course and served as a test group, in the sense that their teachers met with PSSC members during special summer sessions to discuss progress and problems.

One result has been widespread use of the new materials themselves and of the new approach embodied in the course, which now involves more than half the high school physics students in the United States. There are also even more impressive achievements. The program represents a breakthrough in the scope and financing of educational innovation, the end of efforts to attain major goals on shoestring budgets—and the first official recognition that the basic revision of a single course may require the expenditure of many millions of dollars. (Major support came from the National Science Foundation and from private industry.)

The program has influenced activities in many areas. Some of its materials, such as the films and paper-back books, are being used in Harvard Project Physics, another physics course for junior colleges as well as high schools—and it has been followed by similar programs for curricula in chemistry, biology and mathematics. PSSC is now part of the recently formed Education Development Center in Newton, Massachusetts, which is also preparing courses in the social sciences for elementary and secondary schools. In all this work increasing attention is being given to objectives, alternatives, and evaluations—the basic elements of the systems approach.

In other words, the systems approach is already being used or about to be used on a broad front. It is not something foreign to educators and teachers who have had long experience in the shaping of complex cooperative efforts. It is evolving in the context of contemporary public planning, and a highly significant aspect of the trend has been a new emphasis on the role of working together in the planning of human affairs. When it comes to precise and "scientific" planning, we have been far more sophisticated in competing than in cooperating. Systems techniques have been designed primarily to increase the effectiveness of contests and rivalries and conflicts, activities of some value in the pursuit of many military and industrial objectives. But the overriding importance of these activities is less obvious in such areas as medical care, education, and the elimination of poverty. The trend seems to be more and more toward the study of consensus problems, and other group phenomena which may be applicable to public programs.

Above all, the evolution of systems research is a sign of the coming of age of the social sciences. At present many basic research projects are bogged down because there is a lack of social engineers and technicians trained for checking hypotheses about group behavior and capable of reducing the lag between the discovery and the application of new behavioral principles. This may be one of the major roles of the systems specialist. If so, it is clear that education has a great deal to learn from the systems approach—and a great deal to contribute to it.